YOUR PSYCHIC SELF

30 DAYS TO DEVELOP YOUR SIXTH SENSE

Muriel MacFarlane

KENSINGTON BOOKS
http://www.kensingtonbooks.com

KENSINGTON BOOKS are published by

Kensington Publishing Corp.
850 Third Avenue
New York, NY 10022

ISBN 1-57566-328-7

First Kensington Trade Paperback Printing: September, 1998
10 9 8 7 6 5 4 3 2

Printed in the United States of America

To my mother
Mae

ACKNOWLEDGMENTS

I want to acknowledge the kindness of friends Sue Kovach, Martha Moffett and Catharine Rambeau who have been so generous with their time and talents. I wish to thank my agent Noah Lukeman for his good sense in recognizing the merit in this project, and my editor Ann LaFarge at Kensington Publishing who helped me see the work through to completion. Additionally, those who participated in discussion groups, seminars, workshops or, whose serendipitous meeting with me gave me bits of useful information; and those who were willing to patiently listen for years and share in sometimes heated but always stimulating conversations about the enchantment of intuition and the sixth sense, mythology, religion, psychology, philosophy, art, literature, science, various so-called New Age concepts, healing, therapeutic touch and the future: Diana Downs, Steven Goldstrom, Anne Richmond, Phyllis Ross, Betty Chapparrelli, Gladys Nichols, Violet Laskovich, Ruth Thone, Sandi Juni, Dorothy Duffy, Gaye LaMark, Irene Moretti, Earle and Mitzi Staley, Jim and Sheila Milne, Wainetta and Harold Coffman, Chris Fensel, Steven Krolik, Lana Thompson, Cleo Downs, Bill Spivey, Marilyn Tucker, May Helen Hinkel, Neil Shireman, Joan McCamish, Augusta Wynn, Kim Dillard, Barbara Alspaugh, Dr. E. Piscatelli—and some who are now part of the universal consciousness; Dr. Edward Downs, Carol Scott, Dr. Haridas Chaudhuri and Shasta.

CONTENTS

INTRODUCTION

Predicting Your Own Future:
Isn't That Why We All Want to Be Psychic?

There are more things in heaven and earth, Horatio,
Than are dreamt of in your philosophy.

William Shakespeare in *Hamlet*

A $12.5 million jackpot winner!

As reported on a segment of the television show *Extra*, Susanne Henley, a forty-six-year-old construction supervisor in Las Vegas, was listening to the radio on her job when she heard a report that the casinos had installed a $100-per-play slot machine whose jackpots were fed from a pool of money from more than seven hundred other slots.

"The minute I heard that report I had a very strong feeling, you could call it a premonition. I felt just like the guy on the radio was speaking directly to me," she said. "I went right over to the New York-New York Casino, and found someone already playing this megabucks slot machine. The man offered to sell me his place on it," she laughed, "but I just waited until he lost his money and was ready to move on. Then I moved in."

Within just a couple of minutes, Susanne was $12.5 million richer!

Who wouldn't want to have that kind of a premonition and then have it come true? How exciting, to have hidden knowledge and insight into past, present and future events; to know what the new millennium will hold, to know what will occur next—in your career, in your love life—even in world events. To know just where your future lies. To heal yourself and others. To know all kinds of things before anyone else. To have the ability to see into the future and make decisions based on information no one else has. Who wouldn't want to have that kind of power? To be psychic? The answer is, of course, everyone wants it.

Mae—The Psychic

My mother, Mae, was psychic. She had psychic experiences as a child and was never discouraged from talking about them. When she was in her teens she began to take an interest in discovering what she had to do to encourage these experiences and how she could block them from entering her consciousness when she felt they were inconvenient. She learned, as do most naturally fey individuals, that a dreamy relaxed state brought the paranormal easily to her. When she became harried and rushed with the business of everyday living, her access was denied. She later discovered that she could go about her workaday world in a calm manner and be in touch with the paranormal at the same time. This balance seemed right to her because she felt less than whole when she was not in contact with her sixth sense.

I watched her being right in the things she predicted and the things she "saw" about people, and I began having psychic experiences myself. Watching Mae was a learning laboratory for me. Today I do not doubt that there are psychic persons or that psychic events do occur which are more than mere coincidences. I believe that people can communicate telepathically with each other, that it is possible to know about future events, to have déjà vu experiences that are meaningful, and to feel the energy fields of other human beings.

As a child I accepted my mother's psychic ability. I learned to be open to people and ideas that many others saw as different or unusual, and I readily accepted people who claimed to be gurus or mystics. Life in our house was often curious and usually fun. Many of Mae's friends were interested in different philosophies. They told tales of novel paranormal experiences, and we listened attentively to all that they had to say. Mae accepted her psychic ability as normal, often telling me that she had "seen or heard a message" which later turned out to be accurate.

When we both turned around on the street because we heard someone calling her name or mine, but found that no one was there behind us, it didn't seem at all strange to me. She would just laugh and say, "The energy just wants to get our attention because it is going to tell us something." I never questioned what "the energy" was, or where it came from or why it existed, I just accepted it. When I told her of unusual things I had seen or dreamed, she listened seriously and attentively. She knew that my experiences were real. I have always accepted psychic phenomena and the paranormal as a normal part of everyday life.

I spent many childhood hours lying back in a big grassy meadow making images out of the clouds passing overhead. In the winter I would gaze into the flames leaping in the fireplace, seeing knights, castles and fire-belching dragons. My mother encouraged my image-making because she knew that these visualizations were a prelude to accessing that energy she so often talked about.

For my mother, tea drinking enhanced a companionable afternoon or evening. Friends, old and new, drank tea and visited together. They relaxed and laughed—and they altered their brain waves, although my mother wasn't aware of this effect. Her get-togethers always included reading tea leaves, and everyone had a great time. If asked which vehicle was best for accessing psychic information, she always replied that it didn't really matter. "The tea leaves, tarot cards, crystal ball—they are all just ways to focus attention. You can use whatever pleases you but remember, the messages often come in images or sounds so soft that they are almost imperceptible. You must be very aware, listen and look very carefully—at your dreams, at the crystal ball, the cards or the tea leaves—so that you don't miss the messages."

My mother complained frequently about television, not only because it was a waste of time and not really entertaining, but because it presented ready-made images and prevented people from visualizing the world for themselves. She said it kept people in a very limited two-dimensional world that took them farther and farther away from the multidimensional world she knew and loved.

It was not until years later, when I studied psychology, that I realized that she was accessing her *alpha* brain waves whenever she closed her eyes and thought about the images she was receiving. Then I began to understand the things she told me that she needed to do to have a psychic experience.

A tea leaf reading is a convivial and pleasurable experience. My Scottish-born mother's tea-making ritual probably had little to do with the reading of the tea leaves, but it was an important part of the ceremony. The tea had to be made in a brown earthenware pot which was first rinsed out with boiling water. The tea leaves were never measured out; she just pinched some loose leaves between her fingers, selecting black, green or oolong from the varieties kept in an elaborate, mother-of-pearl inlaid tea poy, until she decided she had enough for the number of cups of tea she wanted to make. Boiling water was poured over the fragrant leaves, the lid was put on and the tea was allowed to steep until it was strong enough for drinking. The pot was brought to the table wearing a tea cozy— a padded covering placed over it to keep the tea hot for several hours. We had a number of tea cozies, some of them quite elaborate. One was shaped and decorated to look like a little English cottage. Some were handiwork gifts, edged with rickrack or ribbons.

Guests at our house knew they were there for a reading of their tea leaves, but the drinking of the tea was never hurried; they laughed and told each other stories, gossiped and sometimes sang. They sang songs that were popular at the time, and nostalgic songs that reminded them of the places they had come from. Men often pretended they weren't interested, saying it was just nonsense, but sometimes they would allow themselves to be talked into a reading, and some of them were more fascinated with it than their wives. When the tea was finished, the cup was turned over in the saucer to allow the little liquid that was left to drain away. Then the patterns and images, made by the leaves which clung to the bottom and sides of the cup, were interpreted. My mother explained how this worked: "There is an energy in the world, similar to electricity, which causes that particular person's tea leaves to form those particular patterns, which then can be interpreted."

Someone once asked her if people could read their own tea leaves. "Oh, they surely can," she answered. "They just haven't practiced seeing the images that are present there, making pictures out of the leaves that cluster inside the cup, but they usually can once I point them out." Imagination makes the pictures in the tea leaves come alive, just as it takes imagination to make images out of clouds or from the crackling flames in the fireplace.

Often when my mother met someone for the first time, she would shake their hand and say, "Does the name (and she would name someone) mean anything to you?" The stranger would gasp in amazement and reply, "Why yes, that's my mother (or my sister or my husband)." When questioned, mother would simply say, "I heard the name inside my head, as soon as I touched your hand." I don't recall her ever being wrong, but I do remember her saying, "Accessing 'the energy' requires that you be very available emotionally. It isn't easy for someone who ordinarily holds their emotions back to get the feelings right." Sometimes after an evening of reading tea leaves, she would be very tired, as if she were drained by the experience.

I have never had a conversation with anyone who didn't report—although sometimes with a feeling of embarrassment, some type of paranormal experience—a hunch, a gut feeling, a sense of déjà vu, or a vivid dream that had foretold something that came true. Usually people try to find some sort of logical explanation for these experiences, looking to science or reality to explain what they felt or saw or heard. I have heard people say, when out of the corner of their eye they saw an image which disappeared when they looked directly at it, that it was a trick of the light or shadow, unwilling to admit that it might have been a contact with the paranormal. But I am convinced that everyone has met some part of his or her psychic self, whether they acknowledge it willingly or not.

How often have you hesitated to trust your intuition, worried that you might be wrong if you acted on some subtle perception instead of reasoning out what you should do? How often have you avoided cultivating your psychic capacities, your vibrant and heightened awareness, instead of accepting this deeper source of knowledge and expanding this way of knowing? How often have you ignored, instead of responded to your own highly unusual, often inexplicable intuition? How often has a premonition warned you, but you didn't trust that gut instinct; you didn't listen to that tiny inner voice?

Who Is Psychic?

Maybe you are, if you've ever:

- Had a hunch.
- Had a gut feeling about something or someone.
- Had feelings of déjà vu, thought you had seen a ghost or even a wisp of smoke out of the corner of your eye, or seen an aura around someone's head.
- Needed to get in touch with someone and thought about them, only to have them suddenly call you, as if out of the blue.
- Known who was calling before you picked up the telephone, or what was in a letter before you opened it.
- Had a sudden impulse—a strong feeling that you must do something or go someplace—only to discover that you were absolutely right to have responded to that impulse.

- Had a feeling that someone was in the room with you—a feeling so strong that you were compelled to look around to see who was there.
- Awakened in the morning with a sense of foreboding that something bad was about to happen.
- Had a feeling that there was an emergency involving a child or a relative.
- Known what someone was going to say before they said it.
- Had a premonition or a dream about a future event, perhaps even a national event, that turned out to be accurate.
- Heard someone calling your name when there was no one there.
- Had the solution to a problem come to you in a dream.
- Made a major decision in your life based on a hunch rather than on an analysis of the situation.
- Gone to a strange place and discovered you already knew your way around.
- Gotten so involved in what you were doing that you completely lost track of time.
- Had an imaginary friend.
- Visualized a place or a person clearly and easily.
- Had your dreams come true.

From now on, document these occurrences so you can examine them. Think about what preceded them, so you can try to repeat the experience.

You're on your way!

If you answered even one of those questions with a yes, you have psychic talent, with potential to be developed. As we all know, some have more talent than others, whatever the field. We have all known someone who said, "I just sat down at the piano and played," while others had to take years of lessons. When it comes to psychic talent, some are more gifted, some are aware of it all their lives, other come to it later, but with knowledge and practice, everyone can learn to access their psychic power.

Reasearchers into parapsychology have observed that those who were more imaginative as children, who are able to focus their attention on even the smallest detail, and are able to visualize readily may have more talent for psychic functioning than others. But almost everyone can connect with the paranormal universe if they desire. Most of us have underestimated that potential because no one has shown us how to develop it. Everyone with a little practice can develop psychic abilities.

Paranormal Belief

Belief in the paranormal satisfies some very basic human need. Today's average individual has access to huge amounts of information on every topic imaginable every day, information that would be incomprehensible to the scholars of only a couple of decades ago. No longer do we look to the priest, the rabbi or a spiritual counselor for answers about how to live our lives. Questioning, thinking, no longer willing to follow without asking why, many want to live a life that is not based on belief in a religion that dictates that we must live in a way that guarantees a place in a hereafter, whether or not that way is difficult, incomprehensible or self-limiting. Within our society, there is increasing interest in alternative beliefs. Over the past twenty years, the paranormal has enjoyed a revival in popular culture. Books, articles, movies and TV programs are examining such phenomena as UFOs, the Bermuda Triangle, lost continents, yetis, the Loch Ness monster, crop circles, astrology, levitation, ESP and poltergeists. People are looking, searching, yearning, for a completeness that used to be found in the church, in their culture, in a nuclear family.

All of this interest in the paranormal has been categorized as part of the New Age movement. The so-called hippie generation, the 1960s counterculture movement, rejected conventional standards and customs of society and looked for spiritualism, mysticism and alternative healing, which would serve to reassure that there was order and control in what otherwise would seem to be a chaotic universe. Many writers on the subject suggest that these alternative lifestyles serve to counteract the so-called "existential anxiety" that an absence of traditional belief creates, because there still remains that very basic human need to believe there is something greater than ourselves, something that will bring peace and tranquillity, while still allowing for the rejection of the parental-style authorities of the past.

Joseph Campbell tells us in *The Power of Myth:* "People say that what we're all seeking is a meaning for life. I don't think that's what we're really seeking. I think that what we are seeking is an experience of being alive, so that our life experiences on the purely physical plane will have resonance within our own innermost being and reality, so that we actually feel the rapture of being alive."

I find that the majority of people who believe in the psychic experience and who tap into it regularly are comfortably able to integrate their belief in the paranormal with their religious beliefs. In fact, a belief in the paranormal actually has the effect of rounding out their life experiences, so inundated are many of them with science and technology. These are people who attend church regularly, who have sought the advice of their religious advisors frequently, who have christenings, weddings and funerals—life's ceremonies—within the structure of their churches. And so I have difficulty accepting a sweeping indictment of adherents as suffering from an existential anxiety, a lack of religious connection.

The Universal Experience

Forty percent of those polled by *Newsweek* in 1996 admitted to a belief in the paranormal or supernatural without any scientific proof other than their own view of the world or their own experiences. Why would a belief in psychic ability have survived for centuries if there had not been some sort of verification? Many beliefs, such as the concept that the earth is flat, have been disproved. If, over thousands of years, enough paranormal predictions had turned out to be wrong, believing in them would have vanished as readily as the idea that the world is flat. Apparently, paranormal experience phenomenon has been correct frequently enough for it to continue to intrigue humans for centuries.

It just may be that science's view of the nature of the universe is incomplete. *If even 99 percent of reported psychic phenomena are coincidences, exaggerations or even outright lies, then the other 1 percent is still important and should be examined with an open mind.*

You Can Do It

Expand your horizons by making your own inquiries, become your own researcher, and become confident of your abilities beyond the limits of the five known senses. It isn't necessary to go into a deep trance or change your way of living to experience the paranormal. You don't have to sit cross-legged on a mountain top for years, become a vegetarian, or memorize your very own mantra. You don't have to go Greece and consult the oracle at Delphi. You don't have to figure out what Nostradamus meant, you don't have to consult a fortune-teller, get a tarot reading, or call a psychic hotline. You don't have to buy a crystal ball or join a cult. *In as little as thirty days,* you can learn to make your innate psychic ability work for you. You can, with a little practice, learn to tune in to and trust your own dreams and your own gut feelings.

Most of us have some psychic ability. Learning to use that ability will give us additional ways to experience all aspects of life and our environment and to enrich our lives.

This book will teach you how to develop your own psychic abilities—in *just thirty days.*

ONE

Children and Creativity: Where Did All That Talent Go?

Every child is an artist. The problem is how to remain an artist once he grows up.

—Pablo Picasso

In his autobiography *To Kiss Earth Goodbye,* psychic Ingo Swann, who feels that children have psychic abilities far greater than adults, writes: "The world of children does not match very closely the carefully guarded parameters of the respectable, social adult. No one really cares about the perceptions of the child—only that he should somehow be brought into proper conditioning and respect." We don't really know what kind of human being might evolve if a child were left alone to develop without interference. A great many psychics have reported watching glorious colors sparkling from the edges of both objects and people. They say that as children they observed colors shooting out from people all around them—mothers, fathers, friends and strangers—as well as from cats, dogs, leaves and even from rocks. As might be expected, describing these flares of color usually brought disapproval: one is not supposed to see such things, and parental displeasure was often the result of saying that that one did. Eventually, for many psychics, these brightly colored flares emanating from people and things soon faded from their consciousness. Often many years passed before they felt secure enough to look for them once again.

Brain cells have the capacity to generate recordable electrical potentials called brain waves, which indicate the activity of the cerebral cortex. *Theta* waves, which occur in adults during peak emotional experiences such as creativity and psychic phenomena, are the normal brain waves of children.

As children, very few of us had trouble believing in ghosts and many of us had imaginary playmates. It was easy to color cows purple and make the trunks of trees red. The blunt words of childhood often find disflavor with adults who have learned to practice courtesy and are embarrassed by the child who tells adults exactly what they think or feel. Sometimes, with no obvious reason, children dislike an adult and don't mind saying so,

> A child's playground version of an old poem says:
> *"I do not like thee, Doctor Fell.*
> *Why this is so I cannot tell;*
> *But this I know and know full well,*
> *I do not like thee, Doctor Fell."*
> Thomas (Tom) Brown, (1663–1704)
> Written while a student at Christ Church,
> Oxford University

Perhaps the child in schoolyard version of the poem was responding to something many of us have felt about an adult, sensing something about poor Dr. Fell, his aura, his energy field, something which produced a gut feeling, an instinctive reaction that was not readily apparent to reality oriented adults, but you can be sure that such a child was immediately shushed by horrified and embarrassed parents and told to stop being rude. A youngster, embarrassed or punished for being honest, soon learns that many thoughts and feelings are best kept inside because they are unacceptable.

Children who won't go to bed because of the ghosts or monsters in the closet, or who talk out loud to imaginary playmates, are told that, after a certain age they will grow out of their fears and will be ridiculed for continuing to visit with that imaginary playmate. About the time children start school, when cows can no longer be purple, trees can no longer be red, and coloring inside of the lines becomes a good and required thing, imaginary playmates usually disappear. The child learns that drawings need to be realistic and are praised if they reflect the world as it is seen by adults.

Which of us cannot recall hearing: "Stop daydreaming!" "Look at me when I'm talking!" "Pay attention!" "Didn't you hear me calling you?" "Sit up straight!" All those statements are meant to bring a child out of the fantasy world of creativity to become just obedient, conforming and adult.

Creativity and Play

Research into the psychology of individuals who are exceptionally creative has documented that as children they were often intensely curious about their surroundings. Almost everyone who has made a unique contribution to the world remembers feeling awe about the mysteries of life and has rich anecdotes to tell about efforts to solve them.

By the age of six Wolfgang Amadeus Mozart was an accomplished performer, five short piano pieces he had composed by that age are still being played and admired. He ranks as one of the great geniuses of Western civilization.

Mozart's creative method was extraordinary. His manuscripts show that, although he made an occasional preliminary sketch of a difficult passage, he almost invariably thought out a complete work before committing it to paper. His biographers note that he claimed to have heard in his head all the instruments of the orchestra playing the entire composition, complete and finished, before he ever wrote a note. He is said to have told others that the beautiful music came to him "out of the air."

Steven Spielberg is another example of a curious and creative child. His movies have entertained millions of people around the world as he transformed his own fears and obsessions into films. The director of *Jurassic Park, Raiders of the Lost Ark, Jaws* and *Schindler's List* was a film exhibitor by the age of twelve and as a child he told his classmates, "I'm going to direct and produce movies."

"Steven had a lot of imagination" his father said, "and it was not difficult for him to visualize scary or threatening or frightening things. He could transform the shadow of a maple tree outside his window into a monster with gnarled heads and waving tentacles." While we all could easily transform shapes into monsters, pirate galleons on the high seas or dragons as children, few of us feel free to continue to do so as grownups.

A neighbor remembers that Steven was always surrounded by five or six kids as he told them scary tales and, although they screamed in terror, they soon came back for more. He was allowed to grow up in a narcissistic fantasy world where he was permitted to explore his creativity.

His early fascination with dinosaurs, and the methods to transfer his inner visions to the screen, eventually helped him to become a precocious talent rather than an introverted social outcast.

Michael Crichton, the author of *Jurassic Park* has said that he believes Spielberg is arguably the most influential popular artist of the twentieth century.

Joseph Campbell, in *The Power of Myth,* writes that poets and artists are the shamans of today because they are the ones who keep myth alive. It is essential that myth be kept alive, because that is what enables us to understand the symbolic images in the tales and stories of the past—stories we use to comprehend the world.

When author Robert Fulghum wrote, *All I Really Need to Know I Learned in Kindergarten,* he was, whether he realized it or not, writing about the part of us that already knows what it takes to be psychic. Children know that the paranormal is real; it is only adults who don't. The brain waves of children are normally and more frequently in the *theta* range, and it is while in that range that creativity, experiences with great emotional content, and psychic phenomena take place.

Imaginary Friends

Many creative people, particularly children, have imaginary playmates. Edgar Cayce not only had many imaginary friends—children, angels and adults—but he talked about them to his mother. She not only encouraged Edgar to believe in their existence, but she saw them, too.

Todd's Friend

When Todd was three, he began to tell his mother about his imaginary friend Charity. She was pleased because she had been told that this was not only a sign of intelligence, it was normal for a child his age and indicated creativity. Todd said that his friend came from a place that was very difficult to pronounce and after some struggling with it, his mother understood that he was saying Massachusetts.

"I was a little surprised because I couldn't imagine where he had learned it. We allow very little television in our house, only a few children's shows, but I decided that he must have heard it there. Todd talked a lot about his little friend Charity. I never told him that his imaginary playmate didn't exist. I wanted to encourage the development of his imagination. As he described her, her clothes, the chores she had to hurry home to do, such as get water from a well and make a broom to sweep with, I began to realize that Charity was probably someone living in the seventeenth century. I questioned him again and again about her because there was no way he could have any frame of reference for the things he told me about her. When he talked with Charity I heard him using strange archaic words like "doth," "hath," and "thee." When he began school, he spoke of Charity less and less, until she just disappeared. He still gets very angry if we suggest now that she hadn't been real. To this day I have never been able to discover where he was exposed to so many historical facts, but I sincerely believe that Todd had somehow connected with someone from a different time and a different place."

Mae and Play

My mother Mae always found time to play. She attended countless teddy bear tea parties, crawled under tables draped with blankets to form caves, helped hunt for wild tigers and lions, and looked under the toadstools growing in the lawn for the "little people" we believed lived there. I was the envy of the neighborhood because my mother was the only one who could and would jump Double Dutch with all the kids. She read books out loud with different voices for different characters, and she insisted on wearing purple tennis shoes. Looking back, I realize how much Mae enjoyed life. She was well educated, well read, intensively curious about the world, creative, hugely emotional and loving. Her psychic abilities were just another facet of her life, a part that gave her great joy, which she readily shared.

"Walter of Miracles" Mercado

Walter Mercado, a psychic and astrologer, who is well known on Spanish-language radio and television, states in his book *Beyond the Horizon: Visions of the New Millennium* that, as a child, he was known as "Walter of Miracles" because he could see into people's pasts and futures. He was never discouraged, never told he shouldn't do that—he was, in fact, encouraged to delve into the exploration of the use of these powers he believed he held. Mercado says, "It has been like that for me all my life and I have been immersed in the spiritual world since birth." Walter's understanding parents encouraged their creative child and created an environment in which he was cherished.

It is interesting to see the theatrical display of the adult Walter and wonder how different this world might be if all children were encouraged to expand their curiosity and creativity instead of suppressing them to conform to society's norms.

The New Psychology

At long last, a new breed of mental-health professional is contending that otherworldly experiences are legitimate and commonplace. A study conducted by Andrew Greeley and colleagues at the University of Chicago showed that 42 percent of American adults report contact with the dead, 67 percent claim ESP experiences, and 32 percent report clairvoyance. A Gallup poll showed that an extraordinary 15 percent of all people revived from the edge of death reported the spectacle of the near-death experience in which they glimpsed such generic signposts as beckoning loved ones or a tunnel of light. Professionals on the frontier of the new psychology say that such beliefs should not be dismissed. "Paranormal experiences are so common in the general population," said psychiatrists Colin Ross of Dallas and Shaun Joshi of Winnipeg, Canada, in a recent issue of the *Journal of Nervous and Mental Disease,* "that no theory of normal psychology or psychopathology which does not take such experiences into account can be comprehensive."

Harvard Medical School psychiatrist John Mack told *Omni* magazine, "Psychiatry tends to look for the source of these experiences in the psyches of the people who are affected rather than to acknowledge that something is happening to these people." It may be that psychic experiences are not mental conditions but some kind of objective reality that the world does not as yet understand. Whether it is called extraterrestrial or other-dimensional, psychics may live in a different universe from the one science has declared to be real. Mack speaks of vast philosophical implications for human identity in the cosmos. "There's really a great fear of opening up our world beyond what we know," Philosophers of other times have been able to get outside of the tight structure of the thinking of their era and see themselves more in relationship to the universe. As we are more and more able to do this perhaps we will be able to expand our sense of ourselves and our world.

Be Childlike

If we once knew how to be psychic, but unlearned it in order to become functioning adults, and now we want to relearn it, what can we do?

Central among the traits that define a creative person are two somewhat opposing tendencies: a great deal of curiosity and open-ness on the one hand, and an almost obsessive perseverance on the other. The first step toward a more creative life is the cultivation of both curiosity and attention to things for their own sake. There are a few people in this world who say they have never been bored and they credit curiosity for that. Anything or anyone unknown can be interesting and worthy of attention, you can always learn something new. It doesn't need to be useful, attractive, or precious; as long it is unknown it is worthy of attention.

To be psychic we need to become more childlike so that we will take delight in the unknown. And because there is no end to the unknown, that delight can be endless.

We need to relearn how to have fun. Not mindless party-animal fun, the kind where you drink a lot of beer, trash a hotel room or get into a fight outside a bar, but the fun and delight of simple joy-creating experiences.

Watch a child playing in the park. A toddler can be suddenly transfixed by the sudden sight of a snail on a leaf, or the voice of a baby bird in a springtime nest crying for food. And you can, too.

Keep some toys in your bathtub and sink down in the bubbles as you watch a yellow rubber duck float by. Plan a moonlight picnic and invite a few friends to join you. Take a nap, but before you do, eat chocolate chip cookies in bed. Get some dominoes or blocks and create a castle on the floor in your living room—can you bring yourself to leave it there for a couple of days?

The concept of the absent-minded professor is well known in fiction and fact—people of great learning, creativity and inventiveness, who appear to stumble about through their day-to-day lives. Are they simply absentminded or are they busy playing in their minds, playing with ideas that ultimately result in some inspired concept?

Inventors and Myth

The child Thomas Edison began playing with mechanical and electrical apparatus long before his first important invention. By the time he was twelve years old he was selling newspapers on the Grand Trunk Railway. Using a freight car as a laboratory and office, he experimented with printing presses and other apparatus. By age fifteen, from that same freight car, he was publishing a weekly newspaper of his own. When he saved the life of a station official's child, he was rewarded by being taught telegraphy. It was while working as a telegraph operator that he made his first important invention, a telegraphic repeating instrument.

Friedrich Kekule von Stradonitz, the German chemist who is today considered a father of organic chemistry, was searching for the correct model for the molecular structure of benzene. One night he had a very vivid dream about six snakes in a ring, each swallowing the tail of the next. Upon awakening, he realized he had made an important discovery: benzene was structured in the same hexagonal arrangement as the snakes in his dream, and not in the chainlike linear structure which did not fit the experimental data and which had frustrated chemists of his era.

Many creative individuals who are revered for their original thought and learning, believe that myths—the stories we tell to each other and to our children—serve us in ways that foster belief in, and understanding of, the psychic phenomena.

Psychoanalyst Carl Jung wrote about what he called the collective unconscious, a genetically acquired font of information from the thoughts and experiences, acquired over time, by all people who have gone before us—the thoughts, feelings and memories shared by all humanity. Others later called this concept the universal consciousness, a form of collective energy that contains every thought, every deed, everything that has happened in the past. Because time is not linear in this concept, these thoughts and deeds aren't fixed in present time and it thus gives us access to the thoughts and deeds of the past, the present and the future. Jung, in his later years, played with and seriously studied the *I Ching* and he, like Confucius, said he wished for another lifetime to devote to it.

Joseph Campbell is famous for his writings on myth. He, like Jung, held the belief that all myths and epic tales are stories we need, love and delight in. They are linked to the energy of the universe, of which, he wrote, all things are manifestations.

The introduction to Upton Sinclair's *Mental Radio,* his account of telepathic experiments he carried out with his wife Mary, was written by Albert Einstein, who often said he had a great interest in the paranormal. Einstein wrote, "Time and space are modes by which we think, not conditions in which we live," implying that time and space are linear only in our thinking, but not in the way he perceived the universe working.

Play to Make Contact with Your Psychic Self Potential

My mother always suggested to adults who were interested in the paranormal, "Go to a toy store and buy some toys, the kinds of things you liked to play with as a child." She would always ask, "Can you buy them without pretending to the salesperson that they are for someone else's child? Please try."

Often people would express amazement to my mother, and then dismay. They could play a card game or go to a ball game and watch others at play; they could play tennis or touch football; but serious adults had a difficult time thinking about being silly just for the sake of being silly. "How often," she would say, "have most of us been told *not* to be childish?"

Mae would tell them, "Your first step is to act like a child again." While you are at the toy store, buy a bubble wand and some soap, because later you are going to be using bubbles to help you to learn to visualize. Blow some bubbles for the cat and the dog. See if you can really enjoy yourself when you laugh at their antics. If you add some catnip to the cat's bubble solution, even the haughtiest of cats ought to be willing to play with you. Play with your toys, get down on the floor. If you buy a doll, talk to it, dress it up. Smell your toys, feel them, hear them. If you get a little truck, make putt-putt noises with your mouth as it is running along the hills and valleys of the sofa. Forget you are a serious grown-up with a serious job and serious responsibilities and reenter the make-believe world of your childhood." What Mae didn't say (because she didn't know about it) is that this is what you need to do if you wish to create the kind of brain waves that are necessary for psychic experiences.

Psychic Potential Toys

Make a list of the things you liked to play with best, particularly when you played alone.

Go to the toy stores and purchase:

- Your favorite remembered childhood toy (or its equivalent) [not a game such as Monopoly].

- Bubble solution and a wand.
- Find a time when you can be alone with your toys. Try and recall similar times from your childhood and attempt to recreate the mood, the feelings you experienced then. Enter into the world of your toys.
- Play with your bubbles, both indoors and outside.
- When you are done, examine the experience. Did you feel silly or was it easy to get lost in the experience to lose your sense of time? Were you worried that someone might walk in on you and you would find yourself trying to explain what you were doing? Was this playing difficult to do?
- After you have thought about whether or not you found it easy to reenter your childhood world . . . play again.

TWO

The Body Magnetic and Electric: Are There Revolutionary Ideas About Energy Fields and Other Senses?

Sooner or later every one of us breathes an atom that has been breathed before by anyone you can think of who has lived before us—Michelangelo or George Washington or Moses.

—Jacob Bronowski in *Biography of an Atom*

We have fallen out of touch with the psychic faculties that really ought to be as much a part of our everyday lives as are the physical senses. Those two great monoliths of the twentieth century, Science and Technology, have taught us to believe only in those things which are visible and which can be explained technologically. If you can't hold it, see it, take it, eat it, drink it, drive it, wear it, buy or sell it, it either it doesn't exist or probably it isn't worth having or knowing about. Those who dare to talk about their psychic experiences are often dismissed as New Agers, "touchy-feely" people. They are often met with ridicule or avoided because their ideas are deemed kooky.

Many people mock those who seek an alternative to technology, such as exploring the paranormal, but that only reinforces my belief that they are attempting to bolster their own insecurity because today, at every level of society, millions of people are seeking to escape from these materialistic limitations on their lives. A recent *Newsweek* magazine article reported that Deepak Chopra, one of many current motivational and self-help experts—individuals who not long ago would be considered on the fringe—brings in about $15 million a year. That single fact should go far as an indicator of just how many people are seeking something else, something other than what Science and Technology have provided. They are actively seeking alternative states of awareness, ways to live, to expand their consciousness and enrich their lives.

History

Once upon a time everything in the universe was seen from a mystical viewpoint. People believed in fire-breathing dragons, powerful demons, unicorns, magic of all kinds; the trees had spirits, the earth was flat, mermaids swam in the ocean, and gods hurled bolts of lightning from the sky or turned humans into pillars of salt when they were angered.

Then, individuals such as the astronomer Copernicus, began to alter cosmology. He posited that the earth was spinning on its axis and not stationary. In the historical equivalent of a blink of an eye, Galileo followed with his laws of falling bodies. Next, Newton invented calculus and suddenly, in just a few hundred years, science was busily attempting to explain the entire physical world. The world of angels, miracles, shamans and mystics soon disappeared under a glut of technological information. But science only examined the physical world; it refrained from examining the mystical or supernatural. That left a big unexamined area as the province of those who were religious, spiritual or mystical. As science proceeded to examine and name all the parts and the processes of the world in which we live, people began to feel secure. This huge monolith, now known as Science, was providing us with a system of knowledge by which the universe could be understood completely, and by understanding our world, we could then control it and its behavior. The world was not chaotic but orderly, and within man's mastery.

As we drifted away from our connectedness to the earth, and

to the mysteries of life, many felt a void. It was no longer considered politically or scientifically correct to believe in the existence of such things as miracles or the paranormal.

However, a very large part of the universe is still out there just as big, unexamined and unexplained as ever—and we have a great yearning to connect with this enchantment and magic.

The Paranormal Researchers

In the 1920s, most scholars were extremely wary of psychic research. At that time the paranormal was closely associated with spiritualism and fraudulent mediums. A psychic research fellow at Stanford University, John Coover, used playing cards to test whether or not his subjects could guess correctly those cards held by another; he concluded that they could not and that disproved the concept of telepathy or the paranormal. William McDougall, a British physician and psychologist, arrived at Harvard and although his work was to teach graduate students, he also studied parapsychology. One of his students, botanist Joseph Banks Rhine, would eventually become the father of modern parapsychology. After years of work and the testing of 100,000 individual subjects, Rhine published a monograph in which he coined the term "extra-sensory perception" or ESP. Rhine was able to demonstrate, with his card-guessing and dice-calling trials, consistently positive documentable results. He hoped that his controlled experiments would make the scientific community accept ESP as a normal branch of psychology. However, his work proved to be unrepeatable by other scientists. As in all areas of science, experimental results are considered questionable unless they can be reproduced by independent researchers. When Rhine died in 1980, however, parapsychology was known throughout the world and he had left a legacy of terminology and testing procedures. His work had made the field at least a semi-legitimate scientific undertaking and he had encouraged many others, who might not have done so, to consider a career in parapsychology research.

Through this experimentation with prediction and telepathy, researchers have found that a highly relaxed dream state is the optimum condition for an individual to be in for psychic phenomena to occur—something most practicing psychics already knew. Parapsychologist Charles Honorton designed the *ganzfeld* (German for "whole field") cocoon in an effort to duplicate the conditions most conducive to such a state: The subject needs to be secure, comfortable, relaxed, with as little outside interference and distraction as possible. In this cocoon the subject lies in a darkened room, bathed in a dim red light. Eyes covered, headphones fill his ears with a sound known as *white noise,* which is very similar to the sound of rushing water. Cozy and at ease, safe and protected from outside distractions and external sensory stimulation, the subject then is free to focus on any images that come to mind. In these experiments a sender in another room concentrates on sending images, telepathically, to the cocooned subject in an attempt to learn if this individual can receive these images.

People who have experienced this cocoon say that after a few minutes their physical body may feel very heavy or light, even floating. The mental images vary greatly and some report hearing wind, rain, people talking, music, the sounds of animals, but very few report it as being anything other than pleasant. Results have been varied, but this cocoon remains one of the staples of the parapsychological research world because it is thought to provide one of the best possible environments for telepathic experience.

Do It Yourself Ganzfeld

It is possible to duplicate some of the effects of the ganzfeld cocoon in your own home and with it, speed up your connection to the psychic realm.

Assemble the following:

- Red light bulbs. They are readily available at most hardware or lighting stores or the effect can be created with a red scarf draped over the lamp shade. (Never put a scarf directly on the bulb as it can catch fire.)
- A warm blanket or a sleeping bag.
- Tapes of white noise or tapes known as *beta* or *theta,* or their equivalent. They are available through most New Age stores.
- A light blindfold or cloth to place over your eyes.

Select a time when you won't be disturbed. Cuddle up in your warm blanket, but don't lie down; it is too easy to fall asleep. Put on the tapes, close your eyes, take some deep breaths and focus on some question you would like answered. You should be able to easily reach the relaxed dreamy altered state that is often the prelude to psychic experience. Let whatever comes to mind just float through your thoughts.

Altered States Research

Researchers who have experimented in an area known as Altered States Research (ASR) attempt to show that when we loosen our grip on reality, we open ourselves up to a world of communication deep within our own minds. Many prisoners of war or others placed in isolation, where they have experienced a lengthy period of sensory deprivation, have recorded that they have had fearful hallucinations, have been visited by angels or other entities, or have had life-altering experiences such as a newly found belief in God or the determination to seek a life's goal.

There is plenty of debate, however, about where these communications come from. Many scientists feel that they originate in the subconscious mind of the subject and not from any external force. Examples of this concept are often mentioned in studies of channeling and automatic writing in which the channeler or the subject claims to be no more than the instrument through which an entity communicates.

Lengthy sensory deprivation is known to have adverse effects on even the most grounded individual's mental stability and should not be undertaken without proper supervision.

Researchers have used also hypnosis, biofeedback, drugs and meditation in their efforts to induce altered states in volunteer subjects for such research, with varied results.

Yes—No—Maybe

Today's recognized dean of extrasensory perception research, Princeton's Robert Jahn, says that he has found evidence of psychic phenomena in his random number and remote perception experiments, conducted since 1979 at his Engineering Anomalies Research Laboratory.

However, the National Research Council says that there is no scientific explanation for parapsychological phenomena. Conversely, the U.S. Office of Technology Assessment states in one report that the field of psychokinesis, or movement of objects by the mind, deserves further attention.

Dr. Michael Crichton, who, despite his Harvard Medical School education, gave up medicine long ago to write such screenplays and novels as *Coma, Jurassic Park, Rising Sun* and *Sphere,* says that, after a ten-year academic interest in metaphysical matters he attended the California desert retreat of spiritualist Brugh Joy. There, reluctantly, he began to give credence to paranormal phenomena. He now believes what our society denies: that there are many states of consciousness besides ordinary waking awareness.

Professor A. Sturrock, a professor of space science and astrophysics at Stanford University, is unimpressed by any parapsychological results that do not meet strict scientific research standards. He advocates that everyone should evaluate phenomena that appear to be outside of normal experience on the basis of its scientific merit alone. His strategy includes examining the strongest available evidence of any phenomenon, using data only from original sources, and then dealing with the results in "degrees of belief." This would provide results which can then be characterized by probabilities, rather than black or white statements of fact.

Serious researchers in fields including physical investigation, have spent decades, sometimes their entire careers, following all the proper statistical criteria about probabilities for true scientific research, examining people and events thought to be paranormal. Thousands of reports about research projects which have been undertaken to examine the paranormal are available in the scientific literature, and anyone interested in the subject can explore the topic and read about the work of others at length from a variety of viewpoints. The field is controversial, and debate about its legitimacy will continue.

Disciplines Interested in Paranormal Research

Biologists have studied the paranormal because there are implications that unexplained methods of sensing and experiencing the world could exist. Physicists are interested in discoveries about new concepts in our understanding of space, time and matter. Psychologists are curious about new ways of viewing perception and memory.

A human being is an open energy system. We do not stop at our skins. This fact has wide-ranging implications for all the life sciences because it assumes that the transfer of energy between people is natural, and more importantly, can be a continuous event. What is controversial and of interest to all of them is whether or not there are boundaries in the realm of the mind and in this transfer of energy. Can the human energy system flow unimpeded and then intermix with other energies in a process that is always in flux?

Mae and Scientists

Mae didn't care what any of them wrote or said on the subject of the paranormal. She was well educated, but she simply said, on the subject of psychic experiences, "I know what I know."

She was aware that Asian, Eastern, Native American and the other cultures had long held the concept of the inter-relatedness of the universe. That the concept of vital energy forces which were available through flow, pulsation, rhythm, vibration and synchronicity were not unknown and were much more acceptable elsewhere than to the dominant Western thought.

She was also very aware of those who thought psychic phenomena and other aspects of the paranormal were only for crackpots or worse, for exploitation by charlatans who prey on believers, influencing their decisions and relieving them of their money.

When I pursued an undergraduate degree which included classes in chemistry, microbiology and statistics, she was amused. When I went on to a graduate degree in psychology because of my interest in understanding the mind and perception, she was not at all surprised.

Scientific Protocols

Research scientists must begin with an idea, a concept they wish to study, and then they must devise an experiment, with sufficient data, observations, measurements of those observations that ultimately produce experimental results. They must offer as many hypotheses as possible, devise as many experiments and tests as they can, and then proceed to disprove, to reject if they can, all of their own suggested hypotheses. When finally completed, these results must be quantifiable. That is, the research scientists must be able to provide a statistical possibility that their conclusions are not only accurate but reproducible. This includes experimental controls that would prevent results from being falsified. They must separate all the variables that could possibly influence the results and would thus make them questionable.

They must examine all possible explanations for the phenomena they are studying and then confront each of these possible explanations. Often they may not like the conclusion that is reached. They may have to abandon the original idea or go in an entirely new direction in their research. If the new idea survives rigorous examination, it is granted tentative acceptance. The original premise must be examined from all possible directions, and must still be found to be true. Following that, there must be independent confirmation.

Once a research publishes data in a scientific journal knowledgeable proponents will offer differing points of view. Frequently there will be arguments both for and against the data from those who are considered authorities, but if the data is sound, then the researchers will not waver in their acceptance of the results. After years, sometimes decades, a new theory will be validated.

Mae and Protocols

Mae understood and respected the work of scientists, their use of statistics and reproducible results as proof of the validity of their experiments. She knew they are faced with the challenge of proving or disproving that psychic powers either exist or don't and then, ultimately, how they work if they do exist. Mae was often amused by what these authorities had to say. "I don't care about their random-number or dice-tossing experiments," she would say. She often dismissed the articles she read, "What they don't understand is that there is no emotion in all their protocols and their experimental trials. *All* psychic experience contains emotion, some of it almost exhausting to experience. The overwhelming sadness, the stunning joy, the feeling that comes through when you make contact with that sense." She would shake her head in regret at what appeared to her to be their complete lack of understanding. "There is no emotion in random-number experiments or dice rolling. The only emotion I can see in it is the desire to be correct, an ego involvement, not a very big emotional experience or goal for a psychic." This kind of experiment, in her view, had nothing to do with connecting with psychic energy.

"Furthermore," she would say emphatically, "It is unfortunate, most of the research has been devoted to only what I call the first premise, the *existence* of psychic phenomena. All research scientists believe they must look at that concept first, to discover whether or not paranormal experience actually *is*. Until this first premise is proven, science can't take the next step, which would be accepting the existence of the paranormal and moving on to look at the second premise." Her idea of the second premise? How psychic phenomenon actually *works*.

The Intent

But proving or disproving the existence of a sixth sense is not what this book is about. I begin by admitting my bias: there *is* such a thing as a sixth sense.

I lived a large part of my life with a psychic, my mother. I observed her abilities to be proved accurate time after time. I have spent a lifetime looking at the literature and meeting other devotees. Together, Mae and I attended serious workshops and seminars in places such as Esalan Institute in Big Sur, California, and informal meetings in little groups in storefronts and homes throughout the United States. We met a lot of channelers, magicians, con artists and crazy people. We also met true believers and serious seekers of the truth. We talked to hundreds of people who told us the stories of their paranormal experiences, many of which have been included in this book.

I have tried to examine the subject as objectively as is possible for someone who already believes. I have not looked at the phenomena as a scientist; there are plenty of psychologists, physicists and other paranormal researchers doing that. I don't feel a need to look for proof of the existence of the psychic realm. I have examined it from the point of view of someone who already believes that psychic experiences are real.

It is my intent instead to discover some acceptable explanation for the phenomena and, more importantly, to show people who are not already gifted or talented, but who wish to experience the paranormal, how to do it.

Some Well-Known Believers

Carl Sagan, in *The Demon Haunted-World*, believes that three claims in the field of ESP deserve serious study: (1) that by thought alone, humans can (barely) affect random number generators in computers; (2) that people under mild sensory deprivation can receive thoughts or images "projected" at them; and (3) that young children sometimes report the details of a previous life, which upon checking turn out to be accurate and present information which they could not have known about by their own present-day experience.

It certainly helps to know that Sigmund Freud, the father of psychoanalysis, believed that psychic research was a legitimate scientific pursuit, but was wary of linking himself with what he had once called the "black tide of mud of occultism"; to know that anthropologist Margaret Mead was a strong proponent of paranormal research because she had observed evidence of "special supernatural powers" in the primitive cultures she studied; to read that Carl Jung, the great psychoanalyst, spent the latter part of his life asking a question: Are the *I Ching*'s answers meaningful or not? And he implied that he thought the answer to that question was yes.

But it is more important to me to know that I watched Mae access her sixth sense easily and that the things she reported seeing or feeling or hearing turned out to be accurate.

Psychic Animals

Are animals psychic? Do they have abilities beyond those of humans? Some people seem to think so. Animals are able to respond to stimuli that humans cannot detect. For instance, some birds' hearing is beyond anything humans can hear; they migrate for thousands of miles using navigational skills we still don't fully understand.

Whales, dolphins and other marine animals communicate underwater using sounds that are also beyond the range of human hearing; deep in the sea, animals use bioluminescence, an intricate form of light, to convey the signals necessary for their existence; bats use ultrasonic squeaks to navigate; elephants use sounds that can be heard for miles by other elephants—but not by humans. Many kinds of animals exhibit abnormal behavior prior to volcanic eruptions, landslides, earthquakes and tidal waves. Cats have been known to desert their homes and refuse to be lured back inside for as many as five days prior to such a disaster. A number of other animals migrate hundreds of miles or find their way home after being left behind on trips, possibly using the electromagnetic abilities of their brains as built-in compasses. Studies of the senses of animals suggest that the division between sensory and extrasensory might be a lot thinner than we think.

It has been theorized that senses such as these may once have existed in us but have been lost during the evolutionary process. Perhaps psychic powers can be explained by tapping into what animals still have—these possibly once-viable human abilities.

Incredible Things

Not so long ago, no one would have believed that you would talk into a little gadget in your hand and have your voice almost instantaneously heard thousands of miles away; that a picture could be split into little tiny pieces, transmitted invisibly through space, and then reassembled in our living rooms; that we could make this happen just by pushing a button on a little black box held in our hands, making a blank screen come alive with these reassembled pictures. The Internet has shown us that we can communicate instantly with another person anywhere on the globe. The photos which came back from the little rover on Mars and the ability to converse with the astronauts living on the spaceship MIR prove that instant communication can extend beyond this little blue marble called Earth. The rocket Cassini has gone roaring off to explore Saturn and will be out in space for years, sending back data to broaden our world and possibly stun us out of our present limited concepts of the structure of space, our universe, and infinity.

It was also not so long ago that science asserted that the atom was the smallest particle of matter; now there is a whole science based on the study of ever smaller and smaller subatomic particles. Some scientists now accept the superstring theory of subatomic physics, which states that all matter—*all* matter—exists in ten dimensions and that all matter and energy may be able to interact at subatomic levels.

Incredible things are happening in this world today—things that we accept readily, without questioning, things that yesterday's scientists scoffed at. It was once said that the bumblebee is aerodynamically impossible, but there is it, flying and buzzing around the flowers outside the window. And it wasn't until 1945, when the city of Hiroshima, Japan was destroyed by the atomic bomb, that the phenomenon of nuclear fusion became known.

It has been reported that human DNA vibrates at a rate of 52 to 78 gigaHertz (billions of cycles per second, far too fast for anyone to see). This means that the basic structure of human life, the tiny atoms with their electrons and neutrons whirling around the protons, is in a form of energy that is kinetic. This one fact, with its far-reaching implications for our understanding of the paranormal, may help us understand how we are able to connect with another dimension.

Psychic Waves of Energy

There was a time in ancient history when everything that was not readily understandable was attributed to the gods, who had magical powers. They were responsible for the thunder and lightning, the seasons, and everything else that was a mystery.

If you wish, you too can decide that the paranormal is a gift from the gods—magical, a mystery. Or you can decide that it is not "paranormal" at all, just a whole dimension of reality that is out there, waiting to be explained and understood.

In my own search for answers, I read a lot of hard science. This book will be an attempt to save *you* from wading through all the scientific mumbo-jumbo, and to present an understandable explanation.

Electromagnetism

Researchers who have already examined the "mystery" of psychic energy have looked at electromagnetism as a possible explanation. At one end of an energy spectrum are high-frequency waves such as X-rays, and, at the other end, low-frequency waves such as the radio waves which emanate from distant galaxies. Similar waves might be called "psychic waves," but they have not been found—yet.

Another Dimension

Another concept is the possibility of other dimensions outside those which are presently understood—time and space: If, as mathematicians tell us, we have height, width and depth, dimensions which we can see and measure, and time, which we experience and can measure but not see, there exists the possibility that there could be additional dimensions. One of those could be the dimension of human consciousness. Some mathematicians have suggested that there may be as many as twenty-six other dimensions which could intersect with the four known "hard" dimensions of height, width, depth and time. However, since there is no physical evidence to support the mathematical concept of additional dimensions, this theory, too, remains unproven—for the moment.

The Quantum Theory of Physics

The quantum theory of physics examines the behavior of matter at the subatomic level—where things are so small that not only can they not be seen, they are even too little to measure. At that level, it is not possible to demonstrate that matter even exists; it can only be demonstrated that matter has a *tendency* to exist; that is, there is only a probability or possibility that it exists. Quantum physicists know that matter in this possible world functions by different rules of behavior, but by the laws of that science matter does not possess any properties until those properties can be observed.

Quantum physics suggests that there may be hidden connections in the universe, as yet undiscovered, that might potentially account for the existence of psychic phenomena. It has, in effect, confirmed that the very essence of life is vibratory, not solid.

It may be that this vibratory essence is what the psychic (or intuitive) individual senses when they "read" a person or see their aura.

Newton—a Solid and Separate Universe

Every child learns about Sir Isaac Newton, the seventeenth-century mathematician and physicist who invented calculus and established the modern science of dynamics.

Newton determined that everything on earth and in space is affected by the force known as gravity. He investigated the latest developments in mathematics and the new natural philosophy that treated nature as nothing more than a complex machine. Newton provided us with the model for viewing the world as a gigantic mechanism with pistons, pumps, gears, wheels, cogs and pulleys which could not move without one thing exerting pressure or some type of force upon another. The human body was viewed in the same way—as another solid object within this universe, an intricate machine. It is still seen in this manner by medical science. Arms and legs are seen as solid, with joints whose bending pressure provides the force that moves the next joint, as in walking or lifting. The human heart is viewed as a large pump which drives life-sustaining fluids through the body's plumbing. The result of Newton's theories is that his dynamics provided us with a world of separate solid objects, a world where the motions of the planets above us, the functioning of all bodies and all machines, the action of all fluids, followed his basic laws of nature: a huge mechanical universe.

His theory was developed by others to further explain how the world worked. We learned of a universe of atoms, each of which had a nucleus or center of protons, with neurons and electrons revolving around that nuclear center, just as the planets orbited the sun. This world of solid objects included everything, from the smallest to the largest, from pebbles to mountains, from one-celled amoebas to human beings. Everything that occurred in the physical world had a physical cause—all following Newton's laws of motion.

Until the early twentieth century, this Newtonian view was generally accepted. In fact, many still view our world in this way; solid, unchanging, with definite rules—a very comforting image. Most of us have the idea of our world being made up of solid objects, because we experience it mostly through our senses of sight and hearing in three-dimensional space and linear time. It is comforting to believe that our universe follows Newton's laws; that assures us that a lot of things we already know are true and can be relied on. The sun will rise in the morning; if we push against the floor with our feet, we will walk forward; and when we go to bed tonight, we know that the sun will rise again tomorrow morning.

Gilbert—Magnetism and Electricity

Until 1600, when the research of English physician William Gilbert was published, there was no known scientific study of electrical and magnetic phenomena. Electricity and magnetism were, of course, always "out there" but they were unexplained.

The Greek philosopher Thales of Miletus, who lived about 600 B.C. noted that amber, a resinous substance, became negatively charged when rubbed with a piece of fur. But he didn't have any idea why that happened.

The Greeks, Romans and Chinese all observed that when an iron object was stroked with the mineral lodestone, it was capable of attracting another piece of iron.

This information was not really useful to anyone until about 1200, when a crude magnetic compass was first used for navigation. And it was not until the 1600s that William Gilbert realized that the earth itself behaves as a giant magnet and published the first scientific study of electrical and magnetic phenomena and distinguished between the two actions.

Franklin—Atmospheric Electricity

In the late 1700s, Benjamin Franklin proved, in his famous kite experiment, that the atmospheric electricity that causes thunder and lightning was identical to that shown in a very simple condenser. As a result of his experiments, Franklin came to the conclusion that electricity was a single "fluid" that existed in all matter. Later, others considered the concept of a theoretical "life force." Psychoanalyst and biophysicist Dr. Wilhelm Reich, for instance, believed that orgone, an energy which he believed emanated from all organic matter and permeated the universe, could be captured and used to restore psychological well-being.

Morse and Edison——Transmission of Messages

In the next century, Samuel F. B. Morse invented the first instruments for the transmission of messages by electrical impulses. The Morse telegraph was followed by the spectacular inventions of Thomas Edison, who developed the electric light bulb, electric generating systems, sound recording, and motion picture projectors, all of which have altered and shaped the direction of modern society. Now we all accept the fact that electricity is an energy impulse that can be transmitted from one place to another.

Faraday——Fields of Force

Michael Faraday in the early nineteenth century plotted the magnetic field around a conductor carrying an electric current. He had found fields of force that were able to interact with each other and thus he was able to show that light is an alternating electromagnetic field that travels through space in the form of waves. Thus the Newtonian concept of a universe of solid objects that pushed or repelled each other yielded to Faraday's universe of fields of force. But it was only in the realm of physics that this change in concept was considered to have any effect on the world around us. The average person still saw the universe in a Newtonian way, made up of solid and separate objects, a complex mechanical system in which each object or living thing was individual and separate.

Appleton——Force Waves

The concept of energy fields or force waves is based on the premise that energy is neither created nor destroyed, only transformed. This concept states further that atomic and subatomic particles, at various stages of evolution, make up all substances in the universe and are varying forms of pulsating energy. Force fields are everywhere, pulsating above the earth, inside it and below it.

In 1924 the first successful radio range-finding experiments occurred when physicist Sir Edward Appleton used radio echoes to determine the height of the atmosphere. Thus, radar was discovered. Later radar satellites in the earth's orbit were able to monitor global land and sea resources and sonar, a system based on the reflection of underwater sound waves, was used to study the ocean.

Suddenly radar and sonar—force waves which had always been "out there"—became known and usable.

The discovery of these kinds of force fields led to the new idea that all living matter is enveloped in, and made up of, electromagnetic fields. This concept began to negate the Newtonian ideas of solidity and separateness.

Human Energy Fields—Life Fields of Force

The "life force," or a person's electro/chemical/magnetic response, has been called many things: *vis medicatrix naturae* by Hippocrates, *chi* or *qi* by the Chinese, *prana* by the yogis of India, *ki* by the Japanese, *mana* by the Hawaiians, and *tumo* by Tibetans. Just as blood courses through the veins, they all thought, energy coursed through the human body.

They described its routes by a variety of names; the most familiar of these are the *chakras*. All of these cultures have understood for centuries that the human body has energy fields, and no matter what they called this energy or how they described its properties and its actions, they all believed that energy fields exist and can be manipulated and altered through acupuncture, breathing techniques, or a variety of other practices.

The electrocardiograph or EKG is used by physicians to obtain a visible record of the electrical activity of the heart; the electroencephalograph or EEG records electrical activity of the brain. Electrical activity in the human body is known to produce electrochemical responses within the nervous system through the endocrine glands.

Magnetic Resonance Imaging or MRI is a diagnostic tool that produces images of any part the body, without surgical intervention. The body is filled with small biological magnets which emit electromagnetic transmissions as the MRI "listens."

Quantum Medicine-Bioelectricity

In the new field of quantum medicine (also known as bioelectricity) the healing power of magnetism is achieved through electrodes applied to the skin. These act on energy channels, or acupuncture points, within the body.

Test subjects at three universities in China are being introduced to a new microchip technology which emits an electric field of low intensity. Scientists at these universities believe the human body is a complex electromagnetic/chemical system living in a world of electromagnetic energy fields. Microchips placed at acupuncture points have proved to help lower blood pressure, relieve the discomfort of joint conditions, speed the repair of bone fractures, calm nerves, soothe emotions, and relieve a variety of symptoms from headaches to heart palpitations. In Europe studies are underway in which pure magnetic fields are being utilized to shrink tumors and treat rheumatoid and degenerative arthritis.

Thus the science of quantum medicine is taking us to a new understanding of the concept of energy fields, a concept also essential to acceptance of the possibility of the paranormal.

Einstein—Relativity and a Four Dimensional Universe

Prior to Einstein's theory of relativity, which we all have heard of but few understand, the physical laws which described how our world worked were based on the principles of Newton. In the early 1900s, Einstein theorized that space was not three dimensional and time was not separate. He suggested a four-dimensional universe which is now known as the space-time continuum. His theory means that energy and mass are interchangeable. Things we have thought of as solid are not (mass = energy); everything which appears solid is simply a form of energy moving at a differing vibrational rate (energy = vibration).

He proposed that absolute motion does not exist because no object in the universe is suitable as an absolute frame of reference. He suggested that although two observers moving relative to one another at a constant speed would each observe two identical events, one of these observers might perceive two events as happening simultaneously, while the other would see them occurring in sequence. In other words, it is not possible to specify *when* an event happens without saying *where* it happens.

What this means for the paranormal is that since time is no longer linear, a psychic experience could be something that has already happened, something that is happening here and now or in the future, or something that is only a possibility and might never occur.

Einstein questioned the completeness of his theories, saying that he believed they were only the beginning. His theory of relativity has since undergone further development: In the 1960s physicists extended relativity to include electromagnetic phenomena, now known as the Unified Field theory. This theory proposes that four distinct forces control all interactions in matter: Gravitation, electromagnetism, strong force and weak force.

Currently physicists are attempting to combine these current relativity theories to include all force field interactions in one grand unification, or supersymmetry, theory.

Once that occurs, interacting force fields—including the dimension of the paranormal—could become scientifically acceptable.

Planck—A Multitracked Universe

Twentieth-century physicist and Nobel laureate Max Planck, the originator of quantum physics, wrote that we live in what he describes as a multitracked universe. Planck suggests that, on each track of this varied universe, the rules for time, space and matter are quite different from those on every other track.

In the world of everyday sensory reality, the rules are as we see them and experience them. We know that an hour has sixty minutes. You can agree to meet a friend for lunch at a specified time and understand that time will be the same for both of you. If your friend doesn't show up, he is late, and you both will know it. If you measure your living room for a new couch, you know that it will fit, unless you make a measuring error.

However, in the submicroscopic world of quantum particles, none of this applies. An electron can move from one orbit around the nucleus of an atom to another orbit without ever crossing the space between the orbits. This happens without movement, without measurable time for the crossing, and without the electron becoming a different kind of matter.

If we accept Planck's theory that there is such a thing as a multitracked universe, it seems plausible that there might be a path in this multitrack cosmos for the paranormal. And, just as easily, the paranormal track could conceivably be a place where the rules for time, space and matter are quite different from those of sensory reality, relativity, and submicroscopic particles.

Planck and Einstein—A Multidimensional Universe of Electromagnetic Fields

These abstract theories became the basis for an entirely new field of physics known as quantum mechanics. Eventually they provided the foundation for research in such fields as atomic energy.

In just a couple of hundred years, then, energy and mass became interchangeable and what we thought of as a solid object is really energy vibrating at a rate we cannot see. Space is no longer three dimensional, and time is not a separate entity, but they are connected in a four-dimensional or multidimensional space-time continuum where there might be a track for human consciousness.

Our newly conceived universe is no longer a Newtonian machine with multiple parts. It is a dynamic whole whose parts are interrelated.

Experimental Metaphysics—An Interconnected Universe

Later physicists used the concept of energy fields to propose that all living matter is enveloped in electromagnetic fields and by the twentieth century more advanced quantum and particle physicists had developed some theories, which to some minds, can only be called experimental metaphysics. These newer theories maintain that light is a particle and also a wave; not a real physical wave like sound or water, but a probability wave representing the probability of *interconnections.*

In the 1960s physicist John Bell postulated that subatomic particles are connected in ways that go beyond space and time. Bell's theorem says, simply, that anything that happens to one particle affects another and does not occur in any rigid concept of time, but is immediate.

Einstein limited the universe by saying that it was impossible for anything to travel faster than the speed of light. Bell's theorem suggests that subatomic particles are in some way interconnected, so that it is possible to travel faster than the speed of light in what is now described as superluminal speed.

Nobel prize-winning physicist David Bohm has presented credible arguments for a holographic universe in which information is holographically embedded in a field of space/energy/time. Put simply, each piece of a hologram is an exact representation of the whole and one piece can be used to reconstruct the entire thing. What Bohm is saying is that we can no longer view or analyze the world as Newton did, in separate and independent parts. Ours is "a universe of implicate unfolded and enfolded order" in which everything is immediately connected to everything else and is interdependent. In a unified universe, anything that happens to one particle affects other particles. In such a universe, individuals are inseparable parts of that whole and as such, can connect with its powers.

This experiential metaphysical universe is no longer solid, but is made up of a web of interacting and interweaving energy force fields, vibrating probability waves of light, enveloped in electromagnetic fields. It is a universe where the rules about time and space are different from those we presently understand: a holographic universe, in which every particle can contain the essence of the whole.

A psychic can easily relate to this concept of a universe that consists entirely of vast energy fields, interacting and interweaving with no linear time.

Bentov—The Pendulum Universe

If you are willing to consider the concept that the entire universe is a collection of different kinds of energy fields or waves, moving, flowing, interacting, meeting each other, and pulsating, each at its own rate but in harmony with the others, spreading farther and farther throughout the cosmos; if you are willing to consider the concept that these energy fields can possibly enter and leave our bodies through the energy centers known as the chakras, then you will find the theory of Bentov, a medical inventor, reasonable.

Bentov suggests that all energy moves in actions that are characteristic of the pendulum; that is, swinging back and forth, rotating in an orbit, pulsating concentrically, or turning about itself. When any pendulum reaches its apex of motion and pauses to change direction, he theorizes, it then leaves the dimensions we know and expands into space. When its motion begins again, it reenters these known dimensions. He suggests that, along with everything else in the universe, human beings are pendulums; that we are oscillating rapidly and for a period so brief that it is undetectable. We are also able to expand our energy fields into space. It is Bentov's belief that this accounts for those psychic moments, when a person is able to contact the energy of another dimension.

Jung—Collective Unconscious

Carl Jung, the Swiss psychoanalyst, studied diverse cultures of Mexico, India and Kenya, and drew on his wide knowledge of mythology and history, plus his understanding of dreams and fantasy, to write extensively about what he called "the collective unconscious," a universal pool of knowledge. He believed this pool was a coming together of all the thoughts and experiences shared by all people, independent of culture, independent of time and space, and belonging to all of us. He wrote that this collective unconscious coalesced into "archetypes"—universally understood and accepted symbolic concepts. Jung thought that this collective unconscious might be transmitted genetically from one generation to the next: The American philosopher and psychologist William James in his later lectures published as *Pragmatism: A New Name for Old Ways of Thinking,* argued for a pluralistic universe in which such a subliminal cosmic consciousness could occasionally break through into normal awareness.

Senses—Energy Waves

Pythagoras, the sixth-century mathematician who brought us mathematics and geometry's theorem of right triangles, is said to have believed in immortality and the transmigration of souls. He believed that he had brought into his earthly life the memory of all his previous existences. He also believed, as did many of the other ancient Greeks, that a sixth sense (intuition) was an important part of philosophy. The classical philosophers considered this belief an axiom, a self-evident proposition that requires no proof.

Sometime around 300 B.C. Aristotle classified five senses: hearing, sight, smell, taste and touch, the last of which has a number of subdivisions, including the senses of pressure, heat, cold, contact and pain. These senses all function by responding to a form of energy. Hearing: sound waves; vision: light waves; smell and taste: chemicals; touch: nerve sensors. These five senses can be evaluated by measuring known responses which can be quantified. Since Aristotle's time, these five senses have continued to be regarded as the classical five senses.

Now physiologists have accepted the existence of as many as fifteen additional senses and admit there may be more that haven't as yet been discovered. Sense organs, known as proprioceptors, are buried deep within the tissues of the body, within the muscles, tendons and joints. They transmit information to the brain via the nerves—messages about sensations of pressure, the position of the body, and the amount of bending taking place within various joints, as well as messages concerning equilibrium.

It is now believed that odorless substances called pheromones are transferred to the brain through a minuscule structure in the nose known as the vomeronasal organ. This organ was known about for more than a century but was thought to be no more than a useless vestigial organ. Now it is thought to be a direct pathway to the brain, carrying pollenlike chemicals that, when emitted by one individual, have an effect on another. If newly discovered proprioceptors and sense organs actually exist, it becomes even more plausible that there may be another sense—a sixth: psychic ability or intuition.

Dr. Candace Pert, a neurobiologist, has said that neuropeptides—the chemicals triggered by emotions—are thoughts converted into matter. Appearing with Bill Moyers on public television's *Healing and the Mind,* Dr. Pert said, "Clearly, there is another form of energy that we have not yet understood. For example, there's a form of energy that appears to leave the body when the body dies. There are many phenomena that we cannot explain without going into the concept of energy."

Dr. Richard Gerber, who practices internal medicine in Michigan, believes that humans are made up of light waves which he calls "frozen light" and which only appear to be solid. He writes in his book *Vibrational Medicine* that "each human being is an organized interweaving of many bodies of differing vibrational frequencies and through . . . the chakras and our higher frequency bodies, we are able to assimilate energy and information from the highest levels of being. Due to the limited nature of the physical brain . . . we become locked into the perspective of a seemingly fixed space/time frame. Thus, the multidimensional universe is beyond our undeveloped insight. To a fortunate few with clairvoyant perception, the beauty of these invisible realms can be perceived with great ease. The only thing that seems to limit human potential is its definition of itself."

According to Eastern esoteric literature, we are composed of several "bodies," each more subtle than the other. The etheric body vibrates at a higher frequency than the physical body and thus is perceived differently simply because it is less dense.

Conclusion—A Unified Multidimensional Universe of Force Fields

Facts about human physiology such as its electro/magnetic/chemical makeup, combined with the theories of Jung and James about a cosmic or collective consciousness; Planck's and Einstein's theories about space/time, energy waves and force fields; Bell's theorem that everything occurs everywhere at the same time; Bohm's concept of a holographic universe, where each piece is the whole; Bentov's theory of a human that is constantly in motion, like a pendulum, all can come together to provide a view of a majestic and noble interwoven universe of energy waves in which each individual is no longer separate but is a part of that whole, giving us immediate connections to each other and to the force fields of energy of such a universe—instantaneously.

The Now

Obviously, we are more than flesh and bone, amino acids, enzymes and atoms. Mystics throughout the ages have referred to humans as "beings of light." If we are composed of the very stuff of the universe, frequencies of energy, it is possible that we might be, as Gerber suggests, composed of "frozen light." If it is possible to alter the way in which we get into dynamic equilibrium with the energy forces of the universe, we may find that we can connect easily with the cosmic consciousness. Picture yourself swimming in a sea of vibrating energy, waves of electromagnetic fields, vibrating at frequencies we cannot see or hear!

All the esoteric literature says that we can connect to the paranormal through focusing and intensifying our energy using breathing techniques, visualization and meditation.

These disciplines may condition the physical and subtle energetic hardware of our very sophisticated nervous systems to allow us to gain access to higher levels of information. Such techniques might be equated to a radio; we can learn to selectively tune our minds to specific frequencies of energy. Achieving such specialized states of consciousness will allow us to gain access to information which is enfolded within the structures of these energy fields.

It may be that this universe, consisting of pulsating waves of energy, can bring to each of us an experience which is easily understood and acceptable, one which need no longer be considered paranormal if all experience is interconnected and we can tap into it at any time.

Richard Broughton, director of research at the Institute for Parapsychology in Durham, North Carolina, feels that psychic ability hovers just at the threshold of scientific legitimacy. Dr. Keith Harary stated in an interview with *Omni* magazine that "After 25 years of psychological research and the findings of more than 100 years of parapsychology experiments, [he] cannot point to any evidence that indicates that humanity can objectively be divided between psychics and non-psychics." Whether you believe in the existence of these extra-ordinary people or believe those who claim to be psychic are deluded or fraudulent is unimportant, because in such dismissal of them, you exclude a great variety of inner experiences from your concept of what is normal for people. That denial diminishes your sense of your own potential.

Harary said, "We simply do not know enough about the underlying structure of reality to conclude that the laws of nature are never violated and it is far more likely that we do not fully understand those laws. We should investigate the mysteries of nature with a truly open mind."

Nothing written here is the final truth. Perhaps these ideas and observations will stimulate your thought and speculation about interaction between consciousness and the physical world.

We don't need to understand electricity to use it; all we need to do is flip the switch. If we accept the concept of psychic phenome-

non, we don't need to understand it to use it either; all we need
to do is find the switch to flip.

And that is just what we are going to do.

The Future—In The Millennium

The American Astronomical Society recently announced the
discovery, in deep space, of a building block for amino acids—the
foundation of life on Earth. Scientists at the University of Edinburgh in Scotland have successfully cloned a sheep and other British
researchers have cloned a headless frog; ultimately they will be able
to clone headless humans. The purpose? A headless clone would
be unable to experience pain and therefore could be used to harvest
organs for transplants for those in need. There are wonders just
on the edge of discovery which will have far-reaching implications
for accepting very different concepts about the universe and the
way it works.

Eric Utne, founder of *The Utne Reader,* anticipates that in the
next millennium shamanic journeys for people now in their thirties
will be what rock concerts were for them as teens. It should not
be surprising that millions of people, who will live longer and
healthier lives than any previous generations on earth, have already
begun looking for answers they have been unable to find elsewhere.
These millions may very well open up new frontiers in the study
and exploration of psychic phenomena.

There will be millions of individuals, better educated, with access
to more information than ever before, searching for something
better, something more satisfying than anything they already know.
These millions will be looking for new ways to believe; new ways
to think; new ways to live their lives, new therapies; new magic.
They will be looking toward a future that will provide better answers
to how they should live these ever-longer lives in an ever-growing
technological world. The fact that there will be millions of people
seeking answers may mean that not only will there will be a quantum

leap in what will be available, there may be a quantum leap in what will be accepted. The key to making this happen is taking the time to learn how to make your own extrasensory perceptual skills accessible, so that you will be able to more fully use the hidden or long forgotten potential of your mind, which will bring you closer to tapping into the energy of our multidimensional universe.

You can now easily learn how to find your psychic self.

THREE

Self-hypnosis, Focusing and Visualizing:
Are There Simple Ways to Become Psychic
Without a Lot of Hocus-Pocus?

It is not wisdom to be only wise,
And on inward vision close the eyes,

—George Santayana in *O World,*
Thou Choosest Not

You believe in psychic ability. You yearn to experience psychic phenomena at will. Every once in a while something happens that gives you a slight glance into that world, but it hasn't been enough. Occasionally something unusual happens for which there is no explanation—something that tells you there *is* something to this. What you have experienced is just a glimmer of the paranormal, enough to suggest to you that there's more, but the glimpse is so fleeting that before you can grasp it, it is gone again. What do you have to do to *get* there, to learn how to call upon it at will and then *stay* there? The answer is, with just a little practice of some skills, you can be there any time you desire to be.

As a small child, Uri Geller put his finger into an opening in a sewing machine and the shock hurled him into the air; other psychics say they were hit by lightning, or injured in accidents, and upon coming out of these experiences, they had entered into an altered state of consciousness. Their awareness was heightened and they experienced shifts in time. Literally by accident, they became able to access their sixth sense. These experiences often caused a strong emotional reaction, a tremendous ability to focus for a few moments, altered brain waves, or a strong shift in how they felt about their lives. Most of us would prefer to find our way back to this intuitive skill without experiencing serious trauma. Luckily the detailed reports of what some of these individuals experienced provide clues to the expansion of consciousness necessary to access the psychic.

Altered State of Consciousness

In order to have psychic experiences you must be in an altered state of consciousness.

Your brain is producing electrical impulses all the time. Depending upon what is occupying your mind at the moment, you move from one type of brain wave to another. Each category has its own qualities and characteristics.

To be in an altered state of consciousness, you must lower the operating frequency of your brain from the *beta* frequency we are all in—our brain's normal waking state. In *beta* frequency we think rationally, reason logically, perform concrete problem solving, and carry out routine tasks.

But we need only to close our eyes for a moment to begin generating *alpha* waves. Each time you close your eyes, your brain generates a rapid burst of *alpha* waves, but it is those longer, sustained periods of *alpha* that signify the alert, relaxed and sensitive state in which you will be open and receptive to those signals that represent the paranormal experience. These waves are present during daydreaming, fantasizing and visualization. They are associated with a detached awareness and a receptive mind. They can be induced through hypnosis, self-hypnosis or a trance state, meditation, and listening to certain types of music.

For a psychic experience you need to be operating at this lower frequency, the *alpha* range, or at the *theta* range, which is found in the brains of children, and in adults during periods of creativity, highly emotional experiences, or trance states. When these waves dominate, sensations of pain may be dulled—which explains how certain yogis, who have learned to produce these states at will, can lie comfortably on a bed of nails or endure piercing wounds to their bodies. It is also documented in medical literature that complicated surgeries have been performed with the patient under hypnosis in place of anesthesia.

People who normally have high amplitude *delta* waves are easily intuitive and have learned to trust their sixth sense. Obviously, these waves are often present in large quantities in those who easily receive psychic messages.

Delta waves are present in all of us during deep sleep. They are turned on when the rest of your brain waves turn off and they provide the restorative stages of sleep. They may also be present sometimes in a waking state, in combination with other waves. They are a kind of radar that seeks out and receives information on an instinctive level. To access your intuitive skills, to be psychic, you need to learn to increase your ability to operate in *alpha* or *theta* and stay there for as long as you wish without falling asleep.

Studies have proved that it is possible to control the wave activity of your brain, that you can learn to control and lower its operating frequency, to stop it from its habitual busy work. And just how do you do that? Mostly by learning how to relax on command and to visualize.

But, you might respond, "Relaxing is not so easy to do." We all become tense and stressed out rushing around, taking care of the job, the house, the errands, accomplishing all the things we all need to do every day. However, since the brain normally cycles through the different levels of brain waves throughout the day (except *delta,* the range it is in when you are unconscious or sleeping), you have already been there, particularly just before you fall asleep. Whenever you close your eyes your brain automatically begins to generate *alpha* waves, so you actually already know what these operating frequencies feel like. If you want to kick start those *alpha* waves, roll your eyes upward in your head, as if you are looking at something on the inside of your forehead. Just slowing down, taking a few deep breaths, relaxing the accumulated tension in your neck and shoulders is a beginning. Altered states of consciousness are not mysterious, they are normal. Your brain cycles through them daily on a regular basis.

Prayer, Hypnosis, Self-hypnosis and Meditation

It is often said that the left hemisphere of the brain is the logical side and the right is the creative side. However, the brain is actually integrated, with both sides in constant use. (Meditation and prayer have been shown to improve the balance of the two hemispheres.) Neurological studies of brain waves of psychics and individuals with meditation experience have found similarities. In the process of relaxing, concentrating and focusing, both meditators and psychics have shut down some of the excessive activity of the left hemisphere of their brain, the one responsible for the logical thinking our civilization so admires. This shutting down allows the right hemisphere of the brain, the part that years of schooling and has trained into submission, to come into its rightful partnership, balancing the left.

Many people who pray or meditate daily are aware of the benefits they bring. Some, when they are told to try meditation, react negatively: "I just don't have time," "I'm not religious," "Meditating is just for nuts, it isn't for me," or "I've tried it and I just can't sit still," "I can't concentrate for more than five seconds at a time," "I keep thinking about all the work I need to get done," "It sounds nice but my life is too hectic right now." A frequent response is that, "Meditation is wasting time while thinking about nothing." These people have never really relaxed, don't know how, and would be uncomfortable with the new patterns of neurological response that would result. They don't believe that a person who meditates feels better both during and after the meditation, more in tune with themselves, calmer and more able to face life.

The dictionary definition of meditation is: to ponder, reflect or muse. It doesn't have to involve religion, or prayer, or becoming a yogi, spending forty days traveling in the desert barefoot, meeting the Maharishi, or gazing into a candle flame until your eyes water. Meditation is concentration: we do it every day when we pay attention to what we are doing. Some researchers state that longtime meditators actually rewire their brain's circuitry in a beneficial manner. It appears to work for a great many. For thousands of years individuals have practiced meditation as a way of calming themselves, and have found insight and composure.

Hypnosis or self-hypnosis is defined as being guided to, or putting yourself into, a state of relaxation with *focused* attention that excludes all other activities and people around you. Forget all the stereotypes: Hypnosis is no longer the sort of stunt night club entertainers pull on members of the audience to get them to bark like dogs and otherwise embarrass themselves for the entertainment of the crowd. Many physicians, dentists and mental health professionals use hypnosis to help their patients control pain, quit smoking, lose weight, cure insomnia and reduce performance anxiety. The difference between hypnosis and self-hypnosis is only a matter of who does the hypnosis—a professional coach or yourself. The process and the results can be exactly the same, or even better, if you induce yourself, because there is not that unstated fear of giving control to another. The same is applicable to the word trance. For many it suggests a zombielike state of withdrawal, when actually it is similar to a state of repose in which breathing becomes more regular, the body relaxes, and the mind is open and attentive.

People frequently go in and out of a trance whether or not they're being formally hypnotized; hypnosis just intensifies the effect. When you go to a movie, for instance, at first you are aware of the noises around you, the smell of crunching popcorn, the squeak of seats. Once the movie begins, you gradually become absorbed and soon, as you concentrate on the story unfolding before you, you're in a state of focused concentration. In other words—you are en*tranced*.

Relaxation

If you want to communicate with an altered state, you will do so more quickly if you are relaxed.

It is well known that a muscle will relax more completely if you first tense it. If you have trouble relaxing, if you find that the muscles at the back of the neck (where the majority of people hold their tension) or those in your jaw almost never release, you might want to try this tried-and-true five-minute exercise:

- Lie comfortably on your back with your eyes closed. Begin by inhaling, tensing one leg and raising it a few inches off the ground. Hold for a few seconds and then let it drop to the floor as you exhale. Do the same with the other leg.
- Inhale deeply and tense the muscles of one arm as you raise it a few inches off the ground. Hold for a few seconds, then let it drop to the floor as you exhale. Do the same with the other arm.
- Inhale deeply and contract the muscles of your buttocks as you raise your pelvis a few inches off the ground. Hold for a few seconds and let your bottom drop to the floor as you exhale.
- Inhale deeply and push your stomach out like a big balloon. Hold for a few seconds and then relax your stomach completely as you exhale.
- Inhale deeply and hold that breath with your chest expanded for a few seconds. Relax as you exhale.
- Inhale deeply and bring your shoulders up toward your ears, bringing them together in front of your chest and then push them down toward your feet, relax and exhale.
- Inhale deeply and squeeze all the muscles of your face together, including your eyelids, jaw and mouth. Hold for a few seconds and relax as you exhale.
- Bring your attention to your breathing. Breathe with your

diaphragm, not your upper chest, and gradually allow your inhalations to become a little deeper with each breath.

After you have practiced this relaxation technique a few times, you may find that you are able to get into this state without having to tense and relax each muscle group. You may be able to stop what you are doing, inhale deeply, and tense all your muscles at the same time. Hold for a few seconds and relax as you exhale.

Biofeedback is a method of telling you what your body is doing. You can perform a biofeedback check on yourself by paying attention to the temperature of your hands. When you are tense, they will be cold; as you relax, they will become warmer.

When practiced regularly, relaxation with deep breathing can produce a profoundly calming effect and bring you closer to being able to enter a meditative state with ease.

Self-hypnosis and Meditation

Self-hypnosis or a meditative state make it easier for the paranormal to get through to you.

For those who think hypnosis is some kind of magic, or that self-induced hypnosis isn't possible and doubt that they have ever experienced it, try to recall some occasion when you were fatigued—when you have been driving down the road, and suddenly found yourself at your destination but don't remember the trip or how you got there so quickly. It was as if your brain and your driving were both on automatic pilot. Almost every driver has had this experience, which is the result of the monotonous, repetitive task of driving with the eyes fixed on the road ahead and the regular breathing that accompanies sitting almost motionless in an automobile. You are aware of whatever else is going on in your mind other than the automatic act of steering your car. This phenomenon, known as time distortion, is the experience of the distortion of *perceived* elapsed time. Lots of experienced truck drivers have gone from this state to falling asleep at the wheel. Most of us have known occasions when time seemed either to drag or fly by, depending on how interested we were in whatever was gong on. Time can drag when listening to a lecture on a topic we are not interested in, or fly by when spending an evening with friends. Simple self-hypnosis, a state of being relaxed and intensely aware, can readily be induced at almost any time by fixing your eyes on some point or object, slowing and deepening your breathing, and consciously relaxing the muscles throughout your body.

Tom and Altered Time

Tom, a long-haul trucker, thought he might be losing his mind. On a regular route across the width of the state of Florida from the Atlantic Ocean to the Gulf of Mexico, a trip he regularly traveled at night, he passed fruit groves, wide expanses of planted fields, and not much else. "I listen to music, think about my plans for the weekend and try to stay on schedule," he told my mother.

"There's a town or two and some fast food places and a few truck stops, but for the most part the road is straight, unlit and really tedious. One summer night, about two in the morning, I suddenly saw a woman standing at the side of the road ahead of me. My headlights were shining right in her face and I could see her clearly. She had long dark hair, she was wearing blue jeans and a white T-shirt. When I got within about fifty feet of her she began to walk slowly into the road. She scared the hell out of me! I had to swerve to keep from hitting her and I must have traveled quite a way down the road before I could get the truck stopped. I ended up in a little ditch and I felt really lucky that I didn't roll over. I ran back to the spot where I had seen her and she was gone!" Tom ran his hands through his hair, "I looked in every direction and you could see into the fields, there was no place to hide. I ran back to my truck and got my big flashlight, 'cause now I was thinking maybe I had hit her and she was lying in the ditch at the side of the road. I was sweating like a hog, cursing under my breath and very, very worried. I looked for an hour and never found her!" Tom shifted in his seat, a little embarrassed to be telling this story. "I watched the news for a couple of days, even read the local paper, but there was nothing about a hit-and-run. I finally decided that she must have been able to hide from me and I just hadn't been able to find her in the dark."

Mae waited for Tom to go on, but he seemed lost in thought. "So, what happened next?" she prompted.

"Well," Tom seemed reluctant to go on. "After a while I sort of forgot about the whole thing and then six months or so later, I had the very same experience! The same dark-haired woman, wearing blue jeans and a white T-shirt, right in front of my truck, walking in the road toward me, swinging her arms as she took long strides and looking directly at me. I've seen a deer caught in the headlights, but this woman was nothing like that. She wasn't frozen, she was walking directly to my truck. I swerved, stopped the truck and looked for her, but she was gone again. The next day I made my trip back in the daytime and stopped at the place in the road where I had seen the woman. It was easy to find, I could see the skid marks and the tire tracks in the dirt off at the side of the road. I got out and really searched the area. I must have spent a couple of hours there but I didn't find a thing. I felt too stupid to talk to anybody about it and I finally decided that I really must be going nuts." Tom seemed in a hurry to tell his story now. "In the next couple of months I had to make that same trip often, and two more times I saw her. I have seen her a total of four times and I believe that I must be seeing a ghost or something. The only problem is, I really don't believe in ghosts."

Tom said he had never had a psychic experience, had never heard of déjà vu, and the only interest he had in anything even closely related to the paranormal was watching the *X-Files* on TV. But he was now convinced he was experiencing something from the paranormal. He was scared and looking for reassurance and answers.

Sheepishly, he admitted that he had stopped at a little grocery store, patronized by the migrant farm workers in the area, and asked a few questions, such as, "Had anyone ever been killed at that spot on the road, or were there any tales of somebody missing from around the area?" but no one seemed to know anything useful. That made Tom even more convinced that he was seeing something ghostly, but he didn't want to believe that such a thing could happen to him. "My buddies would laugh me right out the door if I told them this story," he said.

With Mae's help Tom free associated about his experience. He could understand the idea of an altered state, one in which he was actually relaxed and dreamy in the cocoon of his truck cab, eyes focused on the white line in the middle of the road and feeling that he might be falling asleep.

Still, it wasn't easy for him to analyze his experience, and he almost gave up a couple of times. But then he thought about how many times he'd seen his ghost woman and he was determined to solve the puzzle. As he worked on his thoughts about all that he had seen, he eventually came to the idea that the woman had actually looked like someone he'd had a crush on in high school. "I haven't thought about her for years, and I have no idea where she is now. In fact, I never even talked to her, I just adored her from a distance," he said sheepishly. As Tom described Nancy, this girl from his youth, he finally hit on something that seemed to make sense to him. "One of the things I loved about her was that she had this very graceful way of moving, a sort of slow motion walk, like she was sleepwalking." As soon as Tom said that, it was as if a light had gone off in his head. "Sleep, sleepwalking! That's it!"

Finally, Tom had begun to analyze the symbolism. He decided he should try and find out what had happened to Nancy before he gave up on his ghost theory. "Maybe she's dead, maybe she sleepwalked into the street somewhere, was hit by a truck and I saw her ghost!"

"Maybe so," Mae agreed. "Why don't you try to find out what happened to her?"

Tom did contact people who lived in his hometown and found out that Nancy was alive and well, married, the mother of two and living in another state.

"Now," he said when he reported back that Nancy wasn't a ghost. "Maybe I should warn Nancy about a danger for her but somehow it doesn't feel right to me. I just know in my gut that this isn't really about Nancy." What felt right to Tom was what he said next. "I know that the message is for me. I know now the message is personal. I've often felt myself drifting off to sleep at that particular part of the highway. My psychic message or ghost is friendly; it's warning me about that section of the road."

Mae smiled, "I don't believe in ghosts, Tom, but if you are having a psychic experience you should understand that it is often difficult to tell if what you are seeing is past, present or future. The universe doesn't present things to us in the same kind of time as we understand. Long-distance driving can put us into a state of self-hypnosis that is very conducive to an altered state so that psychic experiences can break through to us. Only you can interpret what you saw but I certainly suggest you pay attention to it."

Tom seemed very relieved that Mae didn't think his story was crazy. "I thought every psychic believed in ghosts." He smiled and then thought a moment, "I'm going to take it as a message about the future. That's a dangerous strip of highway and I've been warned."

Stop the Mental Static

Mental static—that constant dialogue with yourself that is going on in your head—is a roadblock to paranormal experience.

You can take yourself through a progressive relaxation which directs you to mentally loosen all your muscles, from feet to head. After about fifteen minutes you will feel light and focused.

You already know that you can hypnotize yourself and you are able to understand the state of focused awareness that is called meditation. Meditation is extremely useful for anyone who desires to make contact with the psychic realm. It helps balance the brain's hemispheres and stops the constant static in your mind that interferes with communication with the paranormal.

Pre-Hypnosis Exercise

Speed up your ability to reach that relaxed dreamy state that makes it easier to access the paranormal.

It is well documented that the mobility of the eyes has a direct connection to the ease with which someone can be hypnotized, although the connection is not entirely understood.

You can fine-tune your peripheral vision which is where psychic images are often first viewed, as just a wisp of matter, like smoke or mist.

- Roll your eyes upward. (The more of the whites of your eyes that are visible, the better candidate for hypnosis you are.)
- Roll your eyes around, ten times to the left and ten to the right.
- Look right and left as far as possible without moving your head.

Prove to Yourself That You Can Meditate

The raisin exercise is used in pain clinics throughout the United States and has been validated by objective documentation with equipment that records reduced respiration rates, decreased muscle tension and altered brain wave frequencies. Its participants experience decreased pain levels and an increase in their ability to focus to the exclusion of other external events. It is a quick trip to seeing how easy it is to concentrate to the exclusion of other stimuli.

- First, open a box of raisins and remove just one. Hold it in your hand and allow it to warm a little.
- Look closely at the raisin in your hand. See its color, its shape, see where the stem was attached to the vine when it was a grape. Turn it slowly, examine the wrinkles on all the surfaces.
- Hold it to your nose; close your eyes; smell it. Can you identify the odor? Does it bring up any memories? Would you know you were smelling a raisin if you weren't touching it?
- Keeping your eyes closed, hold it in your fingertips and roll it lightly between them. What do you hear?
- Now put the raisin in your mouth, but don't chew. Just roll it around on your tongue while your saliva plumps it up. What does it feel like? What does it taste like?
- Now chew thoroughly and slowly, experiencing the differences in the texture before you swallow.
- Still with your eyes closed, consider in what ways this raisin was different from all the other raisins you have eaten over a lifetime. Perhaps for the first time you really saw, felt, smelled and tasted a raisin. Jot down a few notes about the experience.

While you were focusing your attention on the raisin, noticing its most minute details, your breathing was slowing, your brain wave frequencies were changing, and you were directing your attention to a task to the exclusion of all other unconnected events. You were putting your brain waves into *alpha* and possibly even *theta* range.

If you performed the raisin exercise, you meditated. You experienced an altered state of consciousness. It wasn't difficult to do and there wasn't anything mystical about it; you simply paid attention to a task and put your body as well as your mind into a relaxed state.

You may want to repeat this raisin exercise if you are unaccustomed to meditating. You can try different fruits or foods, experiencing each of them completely.

Be aware, however, that you can easily move from meditation to sleep, which you don't want to do. If you find you are drifting off, shake yourself a little, take some deep, rapid breaths, and arouse yourself slightly.

Try meditating for five minutes at a time. You need to be in a comfortable position, one in which you are alert but comfortable. Sometimes soft music helps, because it filters out distracting sounds. You may be surprised to find it a refreshing and enjoyable experience. In addition, paranormal awareness increases, and the answers to your problems and questions will appear as if by magic.

Trance States

There are a number of different words for the various types of trance states. Meditation, contemplation, prayer, hypnosis, visualization, and deep relaxation. The brain wave patterns are the same or very similar for all these variations. Many people who are unaware of the concept of meditation frequently spend time in a state of deep meditation without knowing or even caring what it is called. They may think they are just daydreaming, resting, sitting listening to music, or working in the garden, taking a walking, arranging flowers or painting.

In terms of brain waves, it is the right combination, regardless of the activity you engage in to get there. If you have difficulty letting go of the outside world, and find you cannot concentrate because you keep making mental lists or thinking about something you ought to be doing, want to be doing, are afraid of doing, and you find yourself involved in mental static, pay attention to your tongue. *Every time an unwanted thought comes through, breathe relaxation into your mind, and consciously relax your tongue as you exhale.*

All of us talk in our heads most of the time. If you are thinking, you are preparing to speak—your tongue is ready for action. It will be poised, ready to respond to any of your thoughts. Since we all do this almost all the time, this tense tongue becomes a normal feeling state. When you relax your tongue, you make it more difficult to talk. And that will automatically make it more difficult to keep on thinking.

A mandala, which is a painting or drawing of a symmetrical design, has been used for hundreds of years by mystics and yogis as an object for concentration, but there is nothing mystical about the use of one. They are no more than a series of geometric patterns formed around an ever-expanding series of concentric forms around one central point. These patterns can be easily found in nature, in the ripples that spread out from a pebble dropped in a pond, in the crystalline structures of gemstones, in the convoluted forms of tiny seeds, and in the symmetry of flowers. If you have ever been inside a church and looked at a stained glass window you have undoubtedly found a mandala there. A flower (such as a daisy with its white petals around a bright yellow center, or the traditional lotus blossom that is a feature of so many Eastern religious practices), or a crystal (of any mineral) are all mandalas. You might gaze on your crystal and imagine pure white light spiraling out from it and gradually enveloping your body. The point of having an object as the focus of your meditation is because trying to think of nothing is very difficult. Having an object to observe helps prevent distracting thoughts from taking you away from the meditation. Mandalas, crystals, a flame or a flower are just a few of the traditional vision-fixating objects that help focus concentration. When focusing on a mandala, concentrate on the center of the design and allow the outer designs to be barely visible in your side or peripheral vision. After a few moments your mind will stop attempting to organize the mandala into recognizable structures and will begin to generate relaxed *alpha* waves. If you prefer, you can focus on any repetitive task which relaxes both your body and your mind. Even something as seemingly ordinary as housework or exercise can become a focus of attention, if you concentrate on what you are doing. Whatever you choose, give it your full attention and experience it with all your senses: taste, touch, hearing, sight and smell.

Anyone can give five minutes a day to the discipline of concentration. Consistency is the secret. By regularly attempting to quiet your mind you will at first find frustration and then, with regular practice, a new kind of inner listening. The purpose of meditation is to find the way to contact that universal intelligence that is the gift that comes to the psychically attuned. The route to this mind-quieting relaxation can also come through mantra repetition (a word or phrase that is meaningful to you), progressive muscle relaxation, or guided imagery. There are suitable choices for everyone.

Top athletes regularly experience trance states; they just don't call them that. Tennis player Chris Evert, who went on to win a total of six U.S., seven French, three Wimbledon and two Australian Opens, has told interviewers that, as a child, she was required to sit at the side of the court and gaze at a tennis ball held in her hand for an hour at a time. The point was not punishment; it was focused concentration. After that experience, she would often go on to win her next match.

Jimmy Connors, one of the world's top players in the 1980s, has said that when he was really concentrating on the ball it would appear to him that it was "as large as a grapefruit and floating through the air so slowly I felt as if I could walk to it."

These are testimonials to the power of concentration, which could easily be considered a form of meditation, a trance, although neither of these two tennis champs might have recognized it as such. With concentration, the answers to problems can and will come effortlessly, from the universal consciousness.

Breathing

Slow regular deep breathing is as much a part of meditating and reaching a state of focused concentration as the act of meditating itself.

Becoming psychically attuned is like growing a garden; it flourishes when you give it the space and attention it requires. You will find a natural pace if you don't try to push ahead before you are ready. If you have ever sat and stared at a clear night sky, the big silvery moon, the twinkling stars, searching, yearning for something beyond your earthly mind, you will find that breathing will allow creative perceptions to bring that vision closer and encourage a truly remarkable journey to begin.

In Thich Nhat Hanh's book *The Blooming of a Lotus,* he writes that meditation can be practiced almost anywhere: sitting, walking, lying down, standing, even while working, drinking or eating. If the body is calm, the mind is calm and conscious breathing makes the body and mind one. The breathing carries in itself an image, an image visualized and kept alive during the whole in-breath or out-breath. For example, this great teacher of meditation suggests that you say in your mind as you breathe:

Breathing in, I calm my body
Breathing out, I smile

When you do this with each breath, it is only necessary to focus on the key words; calm/smile—and suddenly the image is no longer a thinking mind, it is only a breathing mind.

Of course, you can substitute any images that are suitable for you. One that many psychics seem to find beneficial is:

Breathing in, I bring the future
Breathing out, I release the past

The way to breathe during a meditation or self-hypnosis is the same way you breathe when you are calm; slowly, evenly, and deeply, from the diaphragm. As you breathe evenly and regularly, your breath takes you into that relaxed state that makes the psychic experience come about naturally, without effort. Breathing in this manner, with your concentration on your own breath, you become more receptive and it becomes easy to slip into a hypnotic state. The process is inconspicuous, so no one will realize you are entering your psychically receptive state as you become quiet and centered. Soon you will find that you can enter this state at will, accessing that powerful sixth sense whenever and wherever you please.

Focusing

In order to access your sixth sense you must utilize the other five senses: sight, hearing, smell, taste and touch.

Studies have shown that psychic information is generally processed nonverbally, often in mental pictures or impressions that convey meaning, rather than in language.

Lawyers, for instance, have learned that eyewitness testimony in a criminal trial is the most unreliable testimony of all. Law professors routinely set up a demonstration of this fact by having a cohort suddenly run into the classroom, "steal" the professor's briefcase, and run out. The ensuing and wildly differing descriptions of the thief given by forty or fifty class members immediately demonstrates the point that individual observational skills are varied and that there will be as many different descriptions of the culprit as there are observers of the act.

To increase your psychic skills you need to increase your ability to focus your attention on minuscule details and thus increase your skill at observation. Psychic images often appear simply as shapes, fragments or shadowy perceptions, sometimes in no more than what might be wisps of smoke, images that fade as soon as they are brought into focus. In order to develop that mental image into something substantial that can be explained or described, it is necessary to locate and detail the small nuances that can be used to describe this invisible world and make it visible.

When asked to describe someone we see regularly but don't know well, most of us reply something like this: "Well, he's tall and a little overweight, kind of good-looking, maybe around forty years old." Asked for more detail, most of us will mention the most obvious feature, such as a large nose or that he wears glasses. We might remember eye color, we could mention something about the quality of his voice, particularly if there was a regional accent, and after that, maybe a particular style of dress.

Studies indicate that more than 50 percent of us would not know the person's eye color, and would be amazed to learn that we had missed height by as much as five inches, weight by as much as thirty pounds. A whopping 90 percent would not mention odor, and even fewer would speak of what the person felt like, even if they had shaken hands or touched a shoulder.

In contrast, to indicate how keenly observational skills can be honed, a Fort Lauderdale, Florida police officer told me about something known as "muscle reading." "Pickpockets use it regularly," he said. "Although they aren't aware of it, most people guard the location of their wallet with involuntary muscle tension. Whether their money is in their hip pocket, inside their suit jacket, or in their bra, when the criminal 'accidentally' bumps into them, most people will instantly betray where their money is hidden."

Once, when I was the charge nurse on the evening shift of a medical-surgical unit at a large university teaching hospital, a cardiologist in his fifties sat down at the nurses' station to make his chart entries. In that lull that sometimes occurs between the end of visiting hours and the patients going to sleep, he chatted with the nurses standing there. He told us that in his twenty years of cardiac practice, he had learned to predict a diagnosis of almost any new patient's heart condition simply by observing their walk when they first came into his office. We didn't believe him. The nurses challenged him to prove it. When patients who were strangers to him strolled up the hall, he would give a diagnosis. Then we looked at the EKG's folded into their charts (most of these patients had been newly moved from intensive care). To our amazement, the doctor was stunningly accurate. Of the ten patients he saw walking in the hall that evening, his diagnosis was 100 percent accurate.

Professional artists say that even when they are not working on something, they are drawing continuously. In restaurants, out on the street, they are always drawing with their eyes. They are constantly observing and learning how the folds of a skirt fall around a woman's legs, seeing the curve of a cheek in the light coming in on it as it is illuminated in different colors from a neon sign in a shop window, watching the light glint off the scissors in the hands of a beautician.

Focusing on External Detail Exercise 1

Draw a circle. Add two little cups on each side to represent ears.

Think of someone you see regularly, perhaps a coworker who isn't in sight at the moment. Using that circle as a blank face, draw a one line shape from ear to ear that delineates that person's hairline.

If you are surprised that you don't know what the hairline of someone you see regularly looks like, don't be. Most people are unable to do so, even for someone they have known for years. Most of us do not see details; we are not as observant as we think we are.

Try paying attention to people's hairlines. Remember, psychic work requires that you be able to pinpoint details and bring cloudy images into reality. After you have done this, try again a week later, after you have had time to *really* look at the hairlines of people you see every day. You should find that your observational skills, your eye for detail, have improved.

Ben and the Blindness Experience

A journalist Ben was asked to blindfold himself for three days and then write about his experiences as a newly blind person. Although he found the experience terrifying and in no way equates it with what it must be like to be truly blind, he says he learned a lot.

"One of the first things that happened," he told me, "was that I found my hearing became extremely acute. I was really listening, I heard subtle sounds in my house I hadn't noticed before. I very quickly identified just where a sound was coming from because I couldn't rely on my eyes to see what had made the noise. I had to rely on my hearing to act as a warning signal of any kind of impending danger."

"What did your wife think of this?" I asked.

"Well," he said with a laugh, "she's used to some of the things I do for a story but she got tired of leading me around."

"Weren't you tempted to cheat by peeking?"

"Oh, yeah," he replied, "and I can't tell you how glad I was to get that tape and blindfold off. It was an exhausting experience. But, you know, by the third day I was experiencing a difference in the taste of food, and I was far more aware of the texture of different foods. I learned to dress by feeling the differences in the shirts against my hands, very fine differences I had never felt before when I put the shirt on against the bare skin of my upper body." Ben laughed. "It's a learning experience I would recommend to anyone."

Test yourself. Try not using one of your senses for a brief period. Close your eyes and walk around your house. Or put in ear plugs and find out just what sounds in your environment you miss.

Focusing on External Detail Exercise 2

Look around the room you are in; now close your eyes. Describe the room in detail, then write your description down without looking back to verify your facts. If you said to yourself, "This is easy, I've been living here for years," you may be surprised.

Did your description include the texture, the shape or the feel of anything, perhaps the couch or chair you are sitting on?

How about sounds and odors?

Now focus on one item in the room you just described, for example, the floor or the carpeting.

If you described it by just saying "gray carpeting," try "wall-to-wall with a close clipped pile, an oblong stain where something has been spilled, four indentations where a piece of furniture was once located, a dead leaf near the doorway."

Psychic Images Occur in Your Mind

You don't really see paranormal things, you "see" them inside your head. Whether or not the psychic impressions are so intense that they seem to be real, they are usually like a movie running in the mind, often vivid but sometimes just an impression barely within awareness. These impressions can create physiological changes such as increased heart rate, elevated blood pressure or rapid breathing. Although the psychics say, "I see," or "I hear," these events take place deep within their minds.

Mary and the Airplane

Mary agreed to take her friend Susan to the airport, although she really didn't want to drive there and was annoyed that Susan didn't just take a cab. She woke that morning with an uneasy feeling, a feeling of foreboding, but she dismissed it, thinking she was just letting her annoyance determine her mood. But as they got closer and closer to the airport, Mary felt more and more uncomfortable.

"I had this terrible feeling in my stomach. I thought I was going to have to pull over and throw up," Mary said. "Susan was chattering away, excited about her trip and all the things she was going to see and do. Vaguely I heard her tell me she would send me postcards along the way. Suddenly, in front of my eyes, just as if I was seeing a movie, I saw Susan's plane at the end of the runway with flames all around the landing gear. I pulled off the road because I literally couldn't see the road."

"What's wrong?" Susan asked Mary, but for a few moments Mary couldn't answer. When she tried to tell Susan about her vision her friend just laughed.

"Oh, Mary, you and that goofy psychic nonsense. I really can't believe that a sensible person like you believes in that stuff."

They argued for a few minutes; Mary begged Susan to not go, but she wouldn't listen. Then Mary couldn't get the car started. Now Susan was mad at her. "Are you nuts?" she yelled, "I'm going to miss my plane!"

When they got to the airport Susan jumped out of the car and ran for her plane. "I found a parking place," Mary recalled, "because I was sure I might have to wait with Susan for the next flight if I really had made her miss her plane. When I got to the terminal, representatives of the airline were explaining to anxious visitors what had happened to that particular flight."

A young rep told Mary, "There's nothing serious to worry about. Everyone got out okay, there were just a few minor injuries."

"Minor injuries!" Mary gasped.

As it turned out, the plane had slid off the end of the runway when one of its wheels collapsed. Because of a small fire, the passengers were evacuated through an emergency chute. Susan ended up in the hospital with a broken leg.

She eventually took her trip and she sent Mary a lot of postcards. Ask her today if she thinks psychic premonitions are nonsense and she will tell you, "I will never doubt Mary again."

Mary's vision is an example of someone whose psychic ability is well-honed. First, she had that feeling of foreboding, without knowing in any kind of detail what it was about. It is possible that later Mary might have "seen" a wisp of smoke, or the shape or outline of a plane, and then she would have had to seek out details to make them into the kinds of images she could translate into a real comprehensible mental picture. Only then could she describe the danger and warn Susan. But Mary actually experienced vivid pictures in her mind. There was no question about what she was seeing and that it applied to Susan and her flight.

Boost Clairvoyance—Visual Images That Occur in Your Mind

- When you think about something that is not immediately in your view, try to think of it in pictures instead of words. If you think of a friend, don't think Harry or Mary, but imagine their face. See them in both black and white and then color.

  Imagine:
- A starry sky. A candle glowing in a dark room. Visualize all the things it lights up, reaching into the dark shadows.
- Leaving work, getting into your car and driving your route home. Can you picture the things on all four corners of major intersections you pass daily?

- Your local mall or shopping area. See the shops to your right as you walk along.
- If you have difficulty with the details of any route you know well, take a slow trip and see if you can be more observant for your next recall.

Sharpen Your Visual Skills

Sharpening your visual skills will help you to see psychic information in clearer pictures. Visual skills are easy to practice, any place at any time. Practice daily!

- At meetings, notice the small, unimportant details about people in the room, such as the laces on their shoes, the condition of their fingernails.
- While you are watching television, study the background sets, the props used to intensify the scene instead of focusing on the actors or the central action the camera is directed toward.
- In the grocery store, look to see what kinds of things others are putting into their shopping carts. Look away, see if you can list more than seven items.
- At night, observe the shapes and outlines you can see from your windows.
- Put the TV on mute and try to read the body language of the actors. Try reading their lips.
- Go to a big department store and pretend you are a detective on the lookout for shoplifters.
- Mentally record your observations as if you were going to be asked to testify at someone's trial.

Boost Clairaudience—Sounds Which Occur in Your Mind

Although the majority of psychic individuals "see" their psychic experiences, some psychic experiences actually take the form of sounds rather than mental pictures.

Experiment with hearing these sounds in your mind:

Imagine:
- A police siren. Hear it growing louder as it comes near you and then fades off in the distance.
- The crack of the bat when it hits a baseball.
- A crowd at a football game.
- A twig snapping underfoot when you walk in a forest.
- The sound of ice skates as they glide across a frozen pond.
- A train signaling at a railroad crossing.
- The difference between the opening sound of your front door and the door to your closet.
- The difference between the deep barking of a big dog and the yapping of a little one.

Jerry and the Whispered Alarm

Jerry's eighty-two-year-old mother was fiercely independent. She lived alone in the same house where Jerry had grown up. Jerry was a serious man, a CPA with his own business and proud of the attention to detail he gave to his business and his clients. He visited his mother often and called her daily right around dinnertime to be sure she was all right.

"You fuss too much, Jerry," she would say.

"I spoke to Mother that evening as usual," Jerry told me, "and she was just fine. I went to bed early because it was tax time and

I was very tired. I went right to sleep. Suddenly I woke up because I heard my mother calling me. I sat up in bed and looked at the clock. It was 2:30 A.M.

"I lay down and tried to go back to sleep, but I couldn't. I thought it was just a dream. I didn't want to telephone my mother and wake her up, but I couldn't go back to sleep. Finally, I put the pillow over my head and closed my eyes. Then I heard my mother again, very softly, whispering my name over and over, 'Jerry, Jerry.' "

Jerry sat up, dialed his mother's house and was alarmed when she didn't answer the phone. "I got up and drove over there," he said. "As I walked up the front walk I could see a dark form at the edge of the porch. It was my mother. She had fallen after suffering a stroke and she was still whispering my name when I reached her side."

Jerry's mother recovered and still lives on her own, despite Jerry's protests.

"I can always call on Jerry," she says, "I don't even need a phone."

What Jerry experienced is called clairaudience. He knew he wasn't really hearing his mother speak to him in the middle of the night, he was hearing her voice urgently calling him in his mind.

Sharpen Your Hearing Skills

Sharpening your hearing skills will help you to hear psychic information in more distinct sounds.

- Close your eyes and listen to all the sounds around you for a few moments.
- Listen to the sounds inside and outside your house and identify them. Some will be familiar, such as the air conditioner or the furnace starting up, or your neighbor's car. Try to pick out details, such as the sounds the furnace

makes as it cools down, or to distinguish the sounds of your neighbor's car from others in the neighborhood.

- Listen to music and pick out the individual voices of the various instruments.
- Listen to (but don't watch) people you don't know being interviewed on television and see if you can hear changes in their voices when questions cause them stress, when they really don't want to answer or when they aren't being truthful.
- If you have a pet and you see it perk up its ears at some sound, see if you can figure out what it is that the dog or cat was aware of before you were.

It is important to learn to distinguish the soft sounds underlying the louder ones, because psychic voices are often barely audible.

Boost Olfactory—Odors Can Accompany or Precede a Psychic Experience

Often olfactory experiences are the prelude to a psychic experience, such as the smell of a particular perfume, the odor of damp earth, or flowers.

Sensitizing yourself to odors will aid you to be alert for a psychic experience and is an essential part of your psychic development.

Imagine:
- The fumes of a big diesel truck ahead of you in traffic.
- Cookies burning in the oven.
- Fresh coffee brewing.
- The odor you would smell passing the open door of a bar early in the morning.
- Your own perfume.
- A bouquet of roses.
- A wet dog.

Sharpen Your Odor Detection Skills

Sharpening your odor detection skills will help you to identify psychic information when the scent is light or unusual.

- When you enter a restaurant, identify the cooking odors.
- Go to the mall and sniff the various perfumes for sale. See if you can pick out any particular ingredients.
- Open the spices in your kitchen. Close your eyes and identify the various spices such as cinnamon, cloves, marjoram.
- See if you can identify any members of your family by odor alone. Sniff the cat and the dog [and don't blame me if now you have to give Rover a bath more often].
- Try to breathe in an offensive odor and then identify what it is about it that you dislike.
- Identify the differences in the way various people or animals smell.

DeeDee and the Mildewed Books

DeeDee, a graphic artist with an advertising firm, was drowsing in front of the huge fireplace in a lodge in Yosemite Valley. She had taken a weekend vacation to contemplate a new job offer. As she sat by a roaring fire with the snow falling outside the windows, she began to feel her head dropping forward as she got sleepier and sleepier, and she jerked herself awake again.

"I didn't want to be snoozing in front of other guests, complete strangers," she said. "I could just imagine I was going to snore and start drooling. Not a pretty picture."

As she stared again into the leaping flames, she was suddenly aware of a strong odor of mildew. "I looked around. Although the lodge is old, it is beautifully maintained. There were bowls of pine cones and wreaths of evergreen everywhere. I couldn't imagine where the smell could be coming from."

There was another woman reading nearby and DeeDee asked her, "What is that I am smelling?"

The woman smiled and replied, "Oh, it's the pine branches, aren't they just delicious? It's so Christmasy. I just love it. It really puts you in the holiday spirit, doesn't it?"

"I knew then that she wasn't detecting the same odor I was, that I was the only one smelling mildew, and it was very strong," said DeeDee. "I was wide awake now and I sat there and thought about the last time I had smelled mildew. It was in the basement of my parents' house in Pennsylvania. I had started down the stairs but the smell was so strong and overpowering that I backed up and decided I didn't need the old box of books I had stored down there." DeeDee smiled, "Suddenly I knew that experience applied to the present—that I had to apply it to my current situation. I had a gut reaction to the smell of the mildew and knew it was very significant. I needed to back up, not go forward into a dark and frightening place. I didn't need to look there for what I needed. I instinctively knew I could now make the right decision. And I did. I turned down what I believed was an exciting career opportunity." She smiled, "The company folded the next year and I would have been out of a job."

What happened to DeeDee was a psychic experience that led her to an intuitive decision, one she was agonizing over and had been unable to resolve. It took the realization that she was smelling an odor from her past, a symbol that only she could understand. By connecting the two, the past and the present, it was possible for her to understand what she needed to do in her current situation.

Boost Touch—Develop Healing Skills and Psychometry

Sometimes, when you are being given a psychic warning, you may have a feeling of tingling at the base of your spine or the hair stands up on the back of your neck.

Some psychics handle objects belonging to an individual to receive feelings or images about the owners. As soon as they touch the object, they get a mental impression or experience physical sensations such as chills or pain.

Imagine:
- The bark of a tree rubbing against the palms of your hands.
- Hot water in the shower beating against your back.
- The feel of a favorite childhood toy as you hold it against your body.
- The fur of your pet, their claws against your bare thigh.
- A cat's rough tongue licking your hand.
- A hug from a loved one.

Liz and a Handshake

Liz, a middle-aged woman who operates a small-town bookstore, told Mae, "As soon as I touch the hand of someone I am being introduced to, I get information. Images flood my mind, and that information is often very different from the smiling face they present as they say, 'I'm pleased to meet you.'

"Now I don't often shake hands because I don't want to get hit with a stranger's emotional life. It can be exhausting."

For years, Liz has handled letters, keys and the jewelry of strangers and from these items learned information about the owners, a method of focusing known as psychometry.

"What kinds of information do you get?" Mae asked.

"Mostly emotional," she replied. "I can sense the emotions of the person who owns the object and silent words fill my mind, or I get impressions which I have to interpret.

"Sometimes people will want to know if their partner is sincere in a relationship, or whether someone can be trusted in a business deal. I usually can get some kind of feeling about the honesty or dishonesty of the owner of an object." Then she laughed. "I sometimes feel like a bloodhound. I haven't been able to help find someone through their possessions, but sometimes I can tell if they have been involved in violence. Once a woman came to me who wanted to find her missing daughter. I felt from the earrings she gave me that the daughter was dead, but I didn't say so—I would never take away anyone's hope. I just said that I thought she might be missing for a long, long time. The daughter was found dead some months later."

Liz shrugged, "I would much rather do psychic healing. I have learned over the years that if I pass my hands a couple of inches above someone's body, I can feel temperature changes that tell me where their illness or injury is located. I can give that person some of my own energy to help them in getting better.

"I don't even need to know what is wrong with them, I just feel for temperature differences. One thing I make really clear though is that they must continue with their medical regime, whatever it is. I'm just giving them a little psychic boost, an extra shot of positive energy from outside themselves."

Liz told us the story of a forty-eight-year-old woman who sought her help. "She had some kind of cancer, I don't even know what kind, and I didn't ask, but she was exhausted. She had been through surgery and chemotherapy and radiation therapy, lots of difficult times. Her cancer was in remission, but she could hardly get through her days, she was so fatigued. When I scanned her body with my hands I sensed there was an extra high temperature in the area of her throat and below the collar bone where a lot of lymph nodes are located. I concentrated my psychic focus in that area and immediately she said she felt stronger, with more energy.

Did I help? I hope so, and she's convinced I did. The last time I spoke with her her disease was still in remission."

Psychic Healing or Therapeutic Touch

Psychic healing or therapeutic touch is used by a variety of health professionals. In an experiment reported in the *International Journal of Parapsychology,* Bernard Grad, a Canadian biochemist, experimented with the laying on of hands in the wound healing of mice. Three hundred mice were cut by the researchers and placed in three groups: one group was allowed to heal without any intervention, one group was given care by medical students, and in the last group, the mice were held by a known healer, Oskar Estebany. The mice held by Estebany showed impressively accelerated wound healing.

In an even more startling experiment, Dolores Krieger, Ph.D., R.N., a professor of nursing at New York University and a pioneer in the modern concept of the art, conducted experiments which documented the effects of healing touch. She conducted her healing experiments not on people, but on vials of blood. She was able to document that the hemoglobin count in the test tube blood was significantly increased after healing touch was administered. By performing these experiments on blood in a test tube rather than on people who might be influenced by the interaction, she was able to avoid what is known as the placebo effect.

Dr. Krieger, in her books, *Therapeutic Touch* and *Accepting Your Power to Heal,* strips away all the mystique and superstition that has surrounded the practice which, since ancient times, has been known as the laying on of hands. Dr. Krieger never actually touches the patient, but uses what she calls an energy transfer. She claims that it provides relaxation, pain reduction and accelerated healing. The technique is used to give conscious direction of natural human energies toward healing. In the final analysis, it is the patient who heals himself. The therapist only acts as a human energy support system until the patient's own immunological system is strong enough to take over. In addition, Dr. Krieger writes: "Therapeutic touch can be used by those who are committed to helping or healing any persons in need. However, commitment to healing is not enough. Important additional qualities are compassion, a sensitive, balanced receptivity to the unstated and often unrecognized nonphysical needs of the client; a readiness to discipline oneself to finely attune the inner "antennae" for messages coming from the farthest reaches of consciousness; and, not least, the willingness to recognize, honestly and objectively, one's own human limitations."

Sharpen Your Touch Skills

Sharpening your touch skills will help you to sense psychic information when you feel objects or people.

With your eyes closed:
- Feel a variety of fabrics, sensing with your fingers the thickness and texture. Try to tell what color something is just by its feel. [Surprisingly, a number of blind people say that they can do just that, feel color, stating that different colors vibrate at different frequencies under their hands.]
- Handle a variety of substances, feel their temperature, whether or not they are rough, smooth, sticky, pliable.
- Hold an ice cube in one hand, a warm washcloth in the other and try to guess the temperature differences.
- Change hands; see whether or not you are more sensitive to touch sensations in one hand than the other.

Taste

Although the sense of taste by itself is rare in psychic experiences, it often accompanies them. Sharpening this sense will aid in your ability to picture images fully.

Imagine:

- Biting into a lemon.
- The taste of coffee.
- The juice of a crisp apple.
- A gooey piece of chocolate.
- An ice cube.

Kinesthesia

Experiencing feelings in your muscles and joints, which are stimulated by body movement, will aid in the fullness of your visualizations and be helpful in creating mental images.

Imagine:

- The sensations you get playing your favorite sport: the feel of the racket or ball in your hand, pedals against your feet, shoes pounding the pavement.
- The feel of sun on your skin and a canvas chair on your back when you sunbathe.
- Sand between your toes and water lapping at your ankles as you walk on the beach.
- Entering a room in the dark and feeling for the light switch.
- Getting a dirty spot or food off your face with a cold wet cloth.
- Wind blowing your hair around as you ride in an open car.
- Turning over when you have gotten tangled up in the bed-clothes.

Visualizing

The majority of psychic experiences come in images, pictures or impressions that take place within your mind. The ability to visualize—to take these invisible experiences that may only be very vague impressions and make them visible or concrete, so that they can be described—is a necessary component to being psychic.

People who are lucid dreamers and can remember those dreams are usually good visualizers. If you dream in black and white with specific objects in color, or if you dream completely in color and are able to remember your dreams, you are already on the way to being a good psychic visualizer. Although many people claim they do not dream, very few do not; they simply have not made the effort to remember their dreams. Sometimes that's because they believe dreams are not important, or sometimes it's because they are accustomed to jumping out of bed after the shock of the alarm clock's shrill noise, and dream images fade before they can pin them down.

Visualizer Test

Some people find it very easy to visualize. To discover if you are one of those,

- close your eyes and imagine a pleasant scene, someplace you already know, such as a sunny beach. If you can see the people, hear the sounds of the surf, smell the suntan lotion, feel the warmth of the sun on your shoulders and taste the salt air, you are already prepared.
- imagine that you are lying on your bed in your own bedroom at home. Picture your room, the windows, the doors, the things that are on the bedside table. Picture someone you know well coming to the door, calling your name and smiling pleasantly at you. Open your eyes. If you are able to mentally picture even a small part of this, you were visualizing.

If you can form a mental still picture but not a moving picture, you are not alone. A lot of people can only see a picture or a single image like a snapshot but are unable to see people moving or talking. Others find that the edges of their visualizations are fuzzy.

If you find that either or both of these things are true for you, you will need to practice some of the exercises until you can visualize a scene and feel comfortable seeing it totally while moving the images and the people in it about.

Do the eye mobility exercises and practice moving everything in your visualization about; look to the extreme left of your scene, the extreme right, look up and down to the top and the bottom of what you are imagining until you feel comfortable that you can easily see all areas of this scene in your mind.

A new field of sports psychology has emerged to study and teach visualization skills and other techniques to world-class and other professional athletes. In the 1988 Olympics, sports psychologist Dr. Shane Murphy was assigned by the U.S. Olympic Committee to teach visualization to the Olympians. More than seventy athletes in a variety of sports requested his assistance. Winners who used visualization regularly include gymnast Mary Lou Retton, diver Greg Louganis and skater Elizabeth Manley. Murphy taught them to mentally go through their entire routines, see themselves winning, accepting the medal, smiling through their tears while the national anthem was being played. The athletes who participated believe visualization helped them, made their preparation better and benefited their performance and skills.

The ability to visualize is a valuable tool in many areas of your life. You can use it to see yourself getting a job, getting married or divorced, winning an award, acquiring a new skill. If you practice, visualizing will enhance your ability to connect with your psychic power.

For those who cannot visualize easily, practice the following exercises to improve your skills. These are some of the exercises that my mother Mae gave to people who wanted to become more psychic. Practicing them will do two things: increase your ability to visualize a variety of colors, and shapes, and improve your ability to use your peripheral vision. As you relax when you practice visualization, you are creating *alpha* brain waves. As you go into deeper relaxation, you are creating *alpha* and sometimes *theta* brain waves, essential for accessing the psychic realm.

Bubble Visualization

In your mind's eye:
- Begin with something that most all of us have done as a child—blow soap bubbles.
- Sit quietly with your eyes closed and take a few deep breaths to relax.
- Recall a time when you were a small child blowing bubbles. Seated on some green grass on a warm and sunny day, look at your hands as you dip the wand into the bubble solution and draw it out. Blow, pursing your lips as the air leaves your mouth.
- Picture a large bubble floating away into the blue sky, floating toward the puffy white clouds above you.
- If you cannot visualize the bubble easily, try for a few moments and then stop. If you need additional help, buy a bottle of bubble solution and a wand and actually blow some bubbles. Watch them float away from you; then immediately close your eyes and recall what you have just seen.
- Repeat the bubble visualization exercise daily. Slowly, you will find that you are beginning to see the bubble clearly in your mind's eye.

Rainbow Visualization

Sit quietly with your eyes closed and take a few deep breaths. Relax.

- Visualize a large bubble. Look for the rainbow of colors that are ordinarily within a bubble.
- Bring in a mild wind and make the bubble move away from you, first to the left, then the right.
- Picture the bubble rising in the air, going up toward the sky because it is the upward eye movement that will bring you more rapidly to a trance or meditative state. As you watch the bubble soaring upward, see if you can change its direction and then its colors, emphasizing one of the colors until you can see it clearly and vividly.
- Continue practicing until you can not only control the movement of the bubble, but can see different colors in it. When you are able to do that you are then ready to add background and people to the scene.

Mountain Top Visualization

Sit quietly with your eyes closed and take a few deep breaths, relax.

- Picture yourself sitting on a mountain top with clouds above you and some blue sky. Make the image as real as possible with all of your five senses involved. Include the sound of the wind and how it feels against your skin, the smell of the small pine trees which surround you, the feel of the ground underneath you.
- Mentally blow some bubbles and make them go up to the clouds and then bounce back down again.
- As the bubbles reach the ground, create a small valley where the bubbles begin to pile up on top of each other. Fill the valley with bubbles.
- Now take some more deep breaths and consciously take your eyes upward, as if you were looking at your third eye someplace within your forehead. This will take you deeper into a state of self-hypnosis.

- Select one bubble from the heap, a large one, and bring it back to rest on the ground in front of you where you are seated on the mountain top. Look into the depth of the bubble and observe whatever you find within it. You may be surprised at what you see. Whatever it is, just look at it nonjudgmentally for a moment or two, then let the bubble go again.

You need to be able to control your visualizations, moving the things and people in them from side to side, up and down, making colors lighter and darker. The more vivid you can make these visualizations, the better. Once you can can do this, you will find that it becomes easier to take yourself into a trance or a relaxed dreamy or meditative state because visualizing requires several things: relaxing, breathing smoothly, looking inside your head with your third eye and creating mental pictures—all a prelude to psychic experiences.

Henry and the Dark Bird

The first time Henry, a stockbroker, looked into his bubble, he was surprised to see a dark bird with white feathers on its chest. For several days he repeated the exercise and that dark bird was always there.

"I described it to friends who were interested in psychic awareness," he said, "and while they all thought it was interesting, no one knew what it meant. I never had much interest in birds before but this prompted me to go to the library and look at some bird books. I discovered I was manifesting a peregrine falcon. I was absolutely amazed! I've never been much of a student either, but I began to do some reading on the subject. I learned that after the Norman Conquest in 1066 the sport of falconry became extremely popular with English nobility. The type of hawk an Englishman carried on his wrist marked his rank. The king carried a gyrfalcon and an earl a peregrine." Henry smiled, "Not only is my ancestry English, this sparked an interest in genealogy. I found I am distantly related to the Earl of Gloucester.

"I now consider this bird to be my guardian, my protector and it gives me great comfort. I visualize my personal peregrine on my shoulder looking out for me every time I leave my house."

What Henry experienced was a quantum leap in his ability to have a psychic experience. For others, it may take time to produce results and to enhance the ability to visualize, to give the impressions that appear in your mind substance, but that is what you are striving to accomplish. Whatever your level of skill, keep on visualizing, as it will bring psychic experiences closer and closer to you.

Emotions

You may have realized by now that you often don't pay enough attention to the texture of things, that you don't notice sounds in the background, that you block them out because they are distractions. You do not incorporate them into whatever is happening at the moment, or you seldom notice odors, unless they are so strong that they are intrusive.

Take a closer look at the way you handle your emotions, because the emotional content of psychic experiences is often very strong. You may have to give yourself permission to be more free, to laugh and to cry more readily, to say how you really feel. To be psychic is to experience empathy and you will want to be receptive and open to the emotion of the messages from cosmos. Most psychics are quite emotional and sensuous.

Sadness and the Princess

At the death of Princess Diana in a Paris auto accident, I heard from a number of people who do not feel they are particularly psychic but who told me that they had awakened that morning to a feeling of overwhelming sadness they couldn't explain.

Dottie, the mother of several small children said, "I woke up crying that morning and there was no reason for it. My husband thought I was sick. I was surprised when I turned on the TV and heard she had been killed. I didn't know much about her, except that she was beautiful. I don't have much interest in the British royal family either but I knew when I heard that she was dead that it explained the emotion I was feeling."

Mona, a pharmacist reported, "I couldn't shake off the sorrow I felt that morning. It wasn't until much later in the afternoon when someone told me about the accident that I really thought about how sad I was feeling. Perhaps I was experiencing the emotionality of the enormous sorrow of all the people in the world who had already heard and were grieving, all at the same time."

When Dottie heard what Mona said she was worried. "Think about the universal effect this collective unconscious can have with such instant worldwide information. Television and the Internet gives information to millions of people all over the globe simultaneously. If millions of people experience the same thoughts and emotions at the same time as the result of a news story or some world event, what might the effect of this be? If psychics worldwide are sensing the emotions of others, it makes you wonder if such things could affect so many people that they might have a global effect— like an epidemic." She paused, "I guess we all better think good thoughts. I don't want to influence the universal unconsciousness, except in a positive way."

Dreaming

A large portion of psychic experiences come in dreams. That should not be surprising because it is in this sleeping state that we generate *alpha, delta* and *theta* brain waves. It is the recollection and interpretation of these dreams that may be difficult, because the information in them may be primarily symbolic. The dreamer has the task of deciding whether to accept the images literally or to decide whether or not they have a deeper symbolic meaning.

Ancient peoples, such as the Hebrews and the Greeks, believed that dreams were direct messages from the gods. Alexander the Great plotted his battles according to the interpretation of dreams and the Bible is full of stories about dreams and their meanings. The Aborigines of Australia and North American Indians all feel that dreams are every bit as important as waking reality.

Today, psychiatrists and psychologists feel that dreams are very meaningful and should be given more attention.

Eileen and Budweiser

Eileen, a young professional woman, woke up with the memory of a dream about a Budweiser beer delivery truck, which struck her as being very funny since she has a little Yorkshire terrier named Budweiser whom she loves dearly. But by the time she got dressed, ate breakfast and headed out the door to work, the details of the dream were fading rapidly.

"All I could remember was that I had dreamed about this big truck with the Budweiser name and logo on the side," Eileen said. "While the dream nagged at me all day, I couldn't remember details and I couldn't imagine why I would dream about this truck. After a while I put it out of my mind and concentrated on my job. After lunch, I still couldn't shake the uneasy feeling I had, so I went home early. I got really rattled when a big delivery truck pulled out into an intersection and a car slammed right into the side of it! Luckily the car wasn't going very fast. I didn't know any of the people involved and I was nowhere close to being the one who would have hit the truck, so I decided my dream hadn't been a premonition about having an accident. When I walked into the house I began calling Budweiser but he didn't come running like he usually does. Then I got worried and began running through the house and that is when I found him. Unconscious. He had choked on a piece of a chew toy. If I hadn't come home early he would be dead right now, and I would be heartbroken, but he's just fine."

"I have to ask," I said, "was it a Budweiser truck in that accident?"

"Nope. But the dream, the truck and the dog, all together, really shook me up. I'd say there was a lot there to give me the message that I better get home and look after my little Budweiser."

Eileen's dream lends support to the theory that dreams, more than any other psychic phenomena, are manifestations of a link between individuals and the collective unconscious of the universe. She had experienced what Jung called synchronicity (and the rest of us call coincidence).

Synchronicity

In the book *Man and His Symbols,* psychoanalyst Carl Jung describes an important concept, one that he named *synchronicity.* This term means "meaningful coincidence," a coming together of outer and inner events that are not themselves causally connected. Jung thought that these meaningful coincidences occurred when there was a vital necessity for an individual to know about, say, a relative's death. He felt that the abnormal random phenomenon occurred when a vital need or urge was aroused. The example given is: If an aircraft crashes before my eyes as I am blowing my nose, this is a coincidence of events that has no meaning. It is simply a chance occurrence. But if I bought a blue dress and, by mistake, the shop delivered a black one on the day one of my close relatives died, this would be a meaningful coincidence. In the psychoanalyst's thinking, that moment of coincidence brings with it a shift in the balance of psychic energy, pushing into our consciousness a gift from the universe's flow of energy. These synchronistic events seem to occur when we need them the most.

The Chinese theories of medicine, philosophy, and even building are based on what they consider to be a science of meaningful coincidences. They do not ask what *causes* what but rather what "likes" to *occur with* what. Synchronicities are an expression of our psychic rapport with the universe, a sign that something more than coincidence is at work. Thus synchronicity makes us aware of things we might otherwise choose to ignore. By attuning ourselves to these coincidences, instead of just ignoring them, we may be awakened to random events that are perhaps meant, by that ever-evolving web of interacting energy that is the collective unconscious of the universe, to cause us to look for their hidden meaning.

- *Pay attention.* You may possibly discover something you really need to know immediately and this is a way of sharpening your sixth sense.
- *Attribute value to synchronicities*—they are significant. You may even want to record them so that you will be more aware, more in tune, more psychic.
- *Relax, focus, visualize, meditate;* turn down the volume on the static in your mind and allow your intuitive voice to be heard.

Boost Dream Recollection

The majority of psychic experiences occur in dream images. You are more likely to dream if you set the stage for dreaming before going to sleep.

- Keep writing materials or a small tape recorder beside your beside.
- Make your bedroom a relaxing peaceful place. It's best not to watch exciting or action TV just before you fall asleep.
- When you feel yourself drifting off, give yourself a message. Tell yourself that you will dream and you will probably remember that dream or fragments of it.

Journaling and Dream Problem Solving

Dr. Louisa Rhine, the wife of the founder of Duke University's Parapsychology Laboratory, Dr. J. B. Rhine, collected thousands of accounts of ESP experiences which came to her through her requests for information published in popular media. In her book *Hidden Channels of the Mind,* she discussed many of the precognitive dreams she was told. Dr. Rhine reported that these dreams were very vivid, often dealt with highly emotionally charged topics, included people to whom the dreamer had strong ties, were memorably intense, and the dreamers found them difficult to shake off when they awoke in the morning.

For most dreamers however, just remembering a dream is difficult. In order to recall your dreams, solve problems through them, and have them stay with you long enough to be recalled and recorded, you must do things that will recall the dream.

- If there is a problem you wish to have help with, lie in bed with your eyes closed and imagine a white circle before your eyes. Inside that circle, "write" your problem (actually see your hand writing out the problem) in the form of a question. Tell yourself you will remember your dream and ask that your question be answered.

- Be specific, state the problem clearly. If you are vague, you may get a vague answer, one that is difficult to understand. For example, instead of writing: What should I do about my boss? Make the problem more specific: How can I make the boss stop (losing his temper) (swearing) (being rude and crude), etc.

- As soon as you awaken, jot down whatever fragments of your dream you can remember. If you have difficulty remembering them, this daily process of recording will help restore elusive images. After you record the dream from the night before, write whatever comes to your mind. Free associate. Your associations to the dream are as important as the dream itself. It is during this free-association process that the understanding of the dream's symbols, the decoding of the dream, will often occur.

- Before you go to bed, review your dream journal and see if you can find any symbols that you can interpret as being meaningful to you.

- As you think more about dreaming, pay attention to the dreams you do have and try to remember them, you will find that you seem to dream more often. Of course that is not true, because we all dream all the time, but when you focus on dreaming the dreams become part of your conscious awareness and you are able to remember them more readily and in more detail.

You will find that as you make the effort to recall your dreams, the vividness of life increases. The places you visit and the people in them may appear to be strikingly beautiful. You may find that you have an incredible feeling of well-being, that you are able to fly, to soar above the planet, to have experiences that are so joyous that they open your thinking to new views of life.

In *The Dream Game,* Dr. Ann Faraday, a leading dream therapist, describes her lucid dreams as "One of the most exciting frontiers of human experience . . . In fact, one of the most thrilling rewards of the dream game is that this type of consciousness, with its feeling of 'other worldliness,' begins to occur much more frequently." These dreams can be thrilling and rewarding. You might even find that going to sleep and experiencing your dreams can become one of the pleasures of your life.

For Thirty Days:

You now have the skills you need. All you need is some practice.

Do not rush. It takes time to find your way back to that psychic child you left behind.

1. Daily alter your brain waves with self-hypnosis or meditation.
2. Daily focus on detail with all of your five senses.
3. Visualize until you can easily see shapes, colors, control movement, and add people and scenery to your images. A combination of emotionality and the ability to imagine things vividly will stimulate your psychic skills.
4. Imprint on your mind the idea that you *will* dream. Begin a dream journal.
5. Observe what happens. First you *will* notice some very small but significant psychic experiences. They will signal that you have tapped into the psychic energy of the universe now that you are capable of doing so.
6. Be aware of synchronicity—those meaningful coincidences that we so often ignore—because within thirty days you *will* experience some.

It does not matter if you have never had a psychic experience, if you have doubted that such experiences really exist, or that you may have scoffed at people who believe in the paranormal. Whether you are a skeptic, a true believer, or only curious about what might happen, try to take a look at what this experience can bring you, because *anything* and *everything* is possible.

Practice. Have fun with it.

Parapsychological experiments conducted at Duke University found that the most important single attribute in individuals who achieved success in extra-sensory experiments was enthusiasm. Acknowledge the honesty of your experiences and recognize them as potential openings into the psychic realm. Be prepared for something unusual to happen. You *will* have a paranormal experience. There *is* synchronicity in your future!

ᖴOUᖇ

Oracles, Shamans and Mystics in History:
What Was *That* All About?

*I have often admired the mystical way of Pythagoras,
and the secret magic of the numbers.*

—Sir Thomas Browne in *Religio Medici*

R adin in *The Conscious Universe* writes that the medieval meta-phor for the universe was a "great organism" and after the scientific revolution that metaphor was replaced by a "great machine." The long-held view of the world as an organic, personal, holistic place of belonging and meaning became less real—only an illusion, the province of philosophy and religion. The side of the world claimed by science involved impersonal concepts like matter and objective measurement. Ultimately that became "reality."

For thousands of years, there had been a belief that some individuals had the ability to see into the future, to have hidden knowledge and insight into the meaning of the past and its significance for the present and the future. Since ancient times most cultures felt the need for contact, through human intelligence, with something greater than themselves, a need to divine the will of the gods through supernatural or paranormal means. No culture, until our present science-dominated one, has doubted the existence of the ability to see into the unknown and gain knowledge about the world as an organic, holistic place, knowledge that provides a sense of belonging and meaning.

Over the centuries, kings paid oracles, shamans, astrologers, mystics and seers handsomely to give them this glimpse into the unknown—the past, the secrets of others, but particularly, to look into the future. They have asked for someone to guide them, to tell them whether or not to embark on a great battle, how to control whole populations of people, how to gain vast riches, how to choose a queen. Some have offered to sell their souls to the Devil for just a little help in knowing what will happen in time that is yet to be, and for assistance in making the things they most desire materialize.

No ancient Roman would have thought of embarking upon a major undertaking unless augurs—members of a college that existed in Rome from the founding of that city—decided the auspices were favorable. It is a well-known fact that Nancy Reagan called upon the services of an astrologer to suggest favorable dates for high-level conferences and other plans while her husband was president of the United States. San Francisco astrologer Joan Quigley reportedly was paid $3,000 a month to schedule Reagan's travel dates, speeches, and surgeries. Quigley reportedly said, "I thought, 'What's the harm?'"

Nancy Reagan has said, "It was something I did to hedge our bets, to try to keep Ronnie from getting shot again."

It may have worked, says Quigley, who often read the President's horoscope hourly. "Ronald Reagan is the first president elected in a zero year to survive his term of office since William Henry Harrison died in office in 1841."

Pagans, Hebrews and early Christians all believed in divination as a way to interpret the will of the gods. An oracle or diviner has figured prominently in the beliefs of all ancient peoples, including the Babylonians and Greeks, considered to have been very advanced and sophisticated. Among the ancient Egyptians all the temples were thought to have been oracular, that is, their worshippers regularly and routinely sought the guidance of the supernatural. Oracles were also used by the Hebrews, as in the consultation of the Urim and Thummin, sacred objects which were carried inside the breastplate of the high priest of ancient Israel. Phoenicians, citizens of an ancient maritime country of southwest Asia, used oracles to tell them what their deities, such as Baalzebub and other Baalim, or the nature gods wanted them to do, how to conduct their lives.

In China the shoulder blades of oxen and the lower shells of tortoises were read and their readings used to make predictions. By the time of Confucius, the text known as the *I Ching* was relied on to provide hints to the future course of the universe.

In other cultures the future could be predicted through the inspection of animal entrails or by studying the activity of birds. Native Americans still have their medicine men and medicine women and elaborate ceremonies to read the omens, including by means of trance states and visions. In other cultures tea leaves or cards are all that are necessary to look into the future. Making predictions from precious books such as the Bible, or gazing into crystal balls, casting stones or sprinkling bags of sacred sand to form patterns on the earth, interpreting dreams and visions induced by herbs and magic mushrooms in religious rituals—it has been apparent for centuries that those who are able to interpret the secret messages hidden therein can wield enormous power in the lives of those who have sought and still seek their advice.

If anyone doubts the power that comes with divination, consider the Greek oracle of Delphi that was celebrated as speaking for the god Apollo. The Delphic priests developed an elaborate ritual which centered on a chief priestess named Pythia. Her utterances were regarded as the direct words of Apollo; private citizens and public officials alike consulted her. The Sacred Way to the temples was lined with structures filled with rich offerings, sometimes as much wealth as could be gathered and presented by the populace of entire cities, in an effort to appease the god and receive favorable predictions. After the Roman conquest, the art and treasures housed there were confiscated by the Romans, notably Emperor Nero.

In our own times, J. Z. Knight, a channeler who claims to speak for a 35,000-year-old warrior named Ramtha, has built a multimillion-dollar empire, attracting famous people who have followed the advice she provides. Followers, including politicians, Hollywood stars and other celebrities, have moved to Washington state to be near this channeler whose advice—in the voice of Ramtha—appears to govern most of the decisions they make about how to live their lives.

In ancient times there was an obvious benefit to having others, including the gods, authenticate your actions. If a battle went terribly wrong, it was a definite advantage for a ruler to have someone else share the blame. Court astrologers and wise men lived precarious lives—they could be executed for a wrong prediction. At the same time, the riches and honors that came with such positions could be well worth the risk. Today, those with powerful personalities or a persuasive message can sell their claimed psychic abilities or astrological skills and reap great financial gains without the serious and life-threatening risks that those ancient shamans faced.

Nostradamus

Nostradamus, the French physician and astrologer, wrote *Centuries,* a collection of prophecies published in 1555. The prophecies appear in vaguely worded, four-line rhyming verses called quatrains. They describe events from the mid-1500s through to the end of the world, which he predicted would come in A.D. 3797. Hundreds of people have studied and interpreted the prophecies in *Centuries,* connecting certain ones with events that have taken place long after Nostradamus's time. The very fact that his prophecies were so vaguely worded has made it possible for readers to give them a widely varying range of interpretation. When his prophecies were published, his fame increased, and countless believers came to see him requesting cures and horoscopes. Historians write that Nostradamus was both clairvoyant and clairaudient, and it is said that he acquired his healing skills from his visions, in which he saw advanced methods of sanitation and medicine. His innovative treatment methods, and his success with patients during the black plague which swept across Europe, earned him a reputation as a gifted healer, adding to his mystique.

He was so famous that Catherine de Medici, queen of France, asked him to plot the horoscopes of her husband, King Henry II, and their children. During his lifetime Nostradamus was one of the most renowned people in Europe. As a top celebrity of his day, he enjoyed enormous fame, wealth and popularity.

Cayce

In the late 1800s Edgar Cayce was just a poor boy from Kentucky, but today he is known worldwide for his books and cures. At age thirteen, while reading his Bible, he had a vision in which a strange woman appeared to him and granted him a wish: He asked to have the ability to help sick children. Because he was very religious, Cayce was uncomfortable with this vision, for he had no way of knowing where it had come from. For a long time, until he lost his voice ten years later, he chose to ignore it. When doctors could not cure him of his mysterious vocal affliction, Cayce turned to hypnotism, which he claimed he already understood. He said he could readily put himself in a trance, and with the help of a local hypnotist he diagnosed himself, prescribed for himself, and was cured. During the next twenty-two years, Cayce performed thousands of medical readings for others in which he diagnosed and prescribed cures using medical terms he had no knowledge of and prescribing cures which, although radical at the time, are now accepted by many practitioners of alternative medicine. His diagnostic accuracy has been estimated at 85 percent, far superior to many of the trained physicians of his time.

Some analysts of Cayce's work have described him as a clairvoyant but Cayce said he felt he was telepathic, tapping into the knowledge of some transcendental mind—perhaps the collective unconscious which Jung described. Cayce called it God's Book of Remembrance or the universal consciousness.

What is remarkable about Cayce is that when he died in 1945, he left behind more than 30,000 recorded readings dealing with the physical ailments or the past lives of his clients. These all remain on file in the Virginia Beach headquarters of the Association for Research and Enlightenment, an organization that preserves his work. Today this organization claims membership in the thousands and study groups are located on every continent. Over one hundred books, which have sold over twelve million copies, have been written about Cayce. One, *The Story of Edgar Cayce—There is a River,* by Thomas Sugrue, states that Cayce "never used his ability except to prescribe for the sick and to give spiritual advice. He never made any public demonstrations of his powers; he was never on the stage, he never sought any publicity; he did not seek wealth." And, he claimed, "I don't do anything that anyone else can't do." It is perhaps because of that humility that millions of people still identify with him, believe that, he was genuine, continue to read his books and books written about him, and buy the many Cayce products available in health food stores today.

Both Nostradamus and Edgar Cayce, who lived hundreds of years apart and on different continents as well as in very different worlds, are remembered and read today because they made written records of their predictions, making it possible for strangers, scholars, and students to read their work. If they had not kept these detailed records, their work, predictions, diagnoses and prescriptions might have faded into the mists of oblivion.

There may very well have been hundreds of other psychics whose work was just as phenomenal, but we know nothing of them because they failed to document their experience. There is a lesson to be learned here: Keep a journal; record your dreams, your telepathic communications, all your other paranormal experiences. That is the only way you can know whether or not you have been accurate, the only way to verify your psychic powers.

Lincoln

Abraham Lincoln, according to his biographer Ward H. Lamon, looked in the mirror in 1860, soon after his election as president, and saw a double image of himself. Lincoln interpreted this to mean that he would be elected to a second term. After the Cleveland newspaper, *The Plain Dealer* published a story about the president's interest in the paranormal, he is said to have replied to a question: "Only half of it has been told. The article does not to begin to tell the wonderful things I have witnessed."

In a later dream related to Lamon, Lincoln told of arriving at the East Room of the White House and seeing "a corpse before me on a catafalque," (a raised structure used for casket viewing), only to be informed by weeping mourners that "The president has been killed by an assassin." It was not much later that Lincoln was shot by the actor John Wilkes Booth at Ford's Theatre in Washington. It is unfortunate that Lincoln did not make any efforts to record what he meant when he said there were "wonderful things I have witnessed."

Churchill

Britain's Prime Minister Winston Churchill is said to have operated on premonition throughout his life. His intuitive powers saved not only him but others on his staff on several occasions. Once, during a wartime visit to an anti-aircraft battery, his driver opened the car door for him. Churchill didn't enter as he normally would have, but went around the vehicle and sat on the other side of his car. A few moments later a bomb exploded so close to his vehicle, near the side where he would normally have sat, that the car was lifted off the ground and almost rolled over onto the passenger side. When asked later by his wife why he had changed his seat, Churchill replied, "Something said, 'Stop!' before I reached the car door. I knew that I was meant to open the door on the other side and get in and sit there—and that's what I did." Again, although it has been said that Churchill operated on premonition throughout his life, there is a record only of the few times he chose to talk to others about it.

Coral—a Psychic Artist

Coral, who lives in a small town in England, calls herself a psychic artist. Coral has been creating what she says are portraits of dead people for four decades. When someone contacts her for a drawing, she meets with them and says she just allows the drawing to flow from her hand automatically. Over the years she has drawn more than 10,000 portraits of deceased family members or other loved ones. When there are photographs available for comparison, which she is never shown, the likenesses are uncanny.

"For some reason," Coral says, "having these portraits drawn by a stranger who never saw the client's mother or brother or husband while they were alive is very comforting. I really don't know how I am able to do it, but most of the people who come to me in distress about losing a loved one seem to feel that somehow, through me, their loved ones are reaching out and making contact. It may be that it helps the individual feel that there is something after death, another life, a hereafter, and this drawing I do is a communication from those who have passed over. For some reason it appears to give them solace."

Divination takes many forms. Every culture and every era has sought this type of contact, whether it be through mediums such as an oracle; haruspication, the inspection of animal entrails; ornithomancy, the study of the activity of birds; the interpretation of dreams and visions. Some methods pass out of fashion rapidly and some regularly reappear. Today the best known include astrology, crystal gazing, interpretation of messages that are hidden in books, especially the Bible; numerology, palmistry, and the reading of tea leaves and cards, such as the tarot.

Mae—Choosing Your Psychic Vehicle

My mother Mae, who preferred to work with tea leaves, spent her Scottish childhood in the small village of Yetholm. Celtic songs, Highland dancing, and the idea that someone could be "fey"— able to see into the future—were natural parts of the environment. As a child she had an imaginary playmate and, because she was an only child, she was not discouraged from talking to that imaginary friend.

I cannot recall a time when she didn't read tea leaves but she said it was only after having her own tea leaves read as a teenager that she came to realize her own psychic abilities. At that afternoon experience she realized that thoughts and images were coming into her mind about the reader.

When as a young woman she moved to Edinburgh, she made new friends, many of whom said they were druids and traveled often to Stonehenge to take part in magical evenings. She enjoyed the convivial atmosphere that was produced when the friends and believers in the paranormal and mystical, all relaxed, laughed, gossiped and drank tea together before the tea leaves were read.

"But it is all a matter of focusing," she'd say, "whether it is a crystal ball, tarot cards or dreams, you are choosing to opening yourself up to the psychic powers that lie beyond the range of normal experience and allowing them to filter through to your consciousness."

When asked about particular vehicles that seemed esoteric to many, such as the *I Ching* or the Tarot, she would patiently reply, "It doesn't matter. They are all vehicles for accessing the powers, but I think that the correct vehicle will find you, not the other way around, and then you will be most comfortable."

The Vocabulary of the Paranormal

You will encounter many descriptive terms as you look for answers in your exploration of the psychic world. Some of the following should be helpful to you:

Auras are intangible but distinctive emanations, or a radiation of energy fields that appear to surround a person. Metaphysically, an aura is the appearance of a person's energy. It is believed that there are seven levels of auras corresponding to the seven chakras of the body which interact with the universal energy. They begin with (1) the physical layer, followed by the (2) emotional layer, then the (3) mental layer, the (4) loving layer, the (5) communication layer, the (6) caring layer, and finally the (7) spiritual layer. People who study auras maintain that while most of us can, with practice, see one or two layers—those nearest to the physical body—it takes much practice to be able to see the others, those which give indications of the person's spiritual well being.

Undoubtedly you have experienced the energy radiating from another person, which is a reflection of their emotional state, such as anger or joy. You did not describe it as an aura because you did not experience it visibly.

One psychic described an aura as a psychic x-ray. It is possible that it is the electromagnetic radiation of the person or a combination of that radiation and other energies. People who see auras say that they change color and are indicative of the spiritual or true energy of the individual, making them as telling of the inner person as if their DNA was exposed to view.

Researchers at New York University have used a device called SQUID (superconducting quantum interference device) to measure the brain's electrical activity several centimeters above the scalp. They have been able to detect the brain's electromagnetic energy with this equipment. According to Karen Gravelle, a biopsychologist and co-author with Robert Rivlin of *Deciphering the Senses: The Expanding*

World of Human Perception, there may be people who can read other's mental state from actually seeing this energy field.

John White in his book *Future Science,* lists ninty-seven different cultures that refer to the phenomena of auras. Although they use different words, such as astral light or halos, they all appear to be referring to the visible energy fields that surround individuals.

Throughout the ages mystics have indicated that the main emotions connected with the colors of the auras are:

> green — love, a healer
> yellow — intellect
> red — anger, pain, passion
> red/orange — sexual passion
> orange — ambition
> lavender — spirituality
> white — truth
> gold — service to humankind
> silver — communication
> black — disease, thwarted ambition
> purple — creativity
> blue — spirituality, calmness, sensitivity
> dark blue — deeper spirituality

There are, of course, shades and hues of these colors with differing meanings, as well as intensity, location, density and intermingling, which is further interpreted by those who practice aura reading.

Automatic writing is sometimes known as spirit writing. The person goes into a trancelike state and then allows their hand to just flow across the page. Some believe that the writing that results is a communication from the dead. Others say that it is from the collective unconscious energy of the universe. Many psychologists believe that this type of written word comes from the person's own subconscious.

Chakras are the energy fields thought to be located within the physical body. There are seven major, as well as twenty-one minor and numerous lesser ones. They are described as whirling vortexes of energy which exchange energy with the universe. The chakras are the same as acupuncture points in Oriental medicine.

Channeling is a relatively new term, but the practice has been around for centuries. However, in the past, those individuals now known as channels or channelers were called mediums, spiritualists or oracles. The particular gift of the channeler is the ability to give control over their bodies and minds to another energy form—a spirit, an extraterrestrial, or some higher being or energy form. These spirits, or voices, are then able to help the channeler's clients by providing them with a multidimensional wisdom that some claim includes access to the mythical Akashik archives, in which the vibrations of every event that has occurred since the universe began are said to be stored.

One very well-known compilation of words that have been channeled appears in the text of *A Course in Miracles,* which was written by two professors of medical psychology at Columbia University's College of Physicians and Surgeons. Helen Schucman and William Thetford's goal in writing this lengthy and complex text was, they said, "to provide a way in which some people will be able to find their own Internal Teacher." Its message has profoundly touched a great many people, because it has become the basis for many study groups, workbooks, audio tapes and classes, as well as the organization for its distribution, the Foundation for Inner Peace.

One channeler, psychotherapist Barbara Brennan, a former NASA physicist, claims to channel a higher being named Heyoan. The being's basic message is that our physical selves are a small part of a larger entity, a soul that exists outside of space/time. Life on the earthly plane is only a temporary state of consciousness, a sort of a schoolroom for the soul, it says. Working through earthly problems enables the soul to grow. When the physical incarnation has finished with the lesson it was given, it goes home to a beautiful place filled with love.

Arthur Hastings, who studied dozens of channelers for his book *With the Tongues of Men and Angels: A Study of Channeling,* was deeply impressed with the psychic quality of his subjects' advice. He wrote, "Whether the entity is a part of their own unconscious, similar to a multiple personality, or whether they connect in some way with a vast pool of knowledge stored in another dimension, I don't know."

Most people who spend time observing channelers at work end up with mixed opinions. "Not one high-minded entity has ever come up with a carburetor design that would improve gas mileage, something that would concretely help civilization," notes Charles Tart, author of *Open Mind, Discriminating Mind*. "Still, much of what they say is good common sense. It is attribution to an exotic source that makes us more likely to pay attention to the message."

There are those who are of the opinion that the channeler is not faking, but believe that these individuals are tapping into their own subconscious and are sincerely unaware that this is where the messages originate.

Clairaudience (clear hearing) is the ability to hear sounds through extrasensory means. Many psychics state that they hear messages from another realm within their own mind.

Clairsentience (clear sensing) is to perceive information from physical touch through extrasensory means. This includes psychometry and healing.

Clairvoyance (clear seeing) is the ability to perceive events or objects beyond the range of the senses. It is a form of extrasensory perception or ESP in which information is gained through psychic means, rather than through the physical senses. Usually this is done in a trance state during which the clairvoyant describes objects or events which appear only in her mind. Some people believe that clairvoyant experiences come through communication with spirits, while others believe that they come through telepathy, from other minds. Yet another explanation is that the information breaks through from a universal font of knowledge that is accessible to everyone if they would only tap into it.

Collective unconscious is a term used by Swiss psychoanalyst Carl Jung to describe a part of the unconscious mind that is shared by all humankind. He believed that it contained information that is a product of ancestral experience and is a remnant of the infinite past. This has been expanded by others to describe a universal force that is thought to contain all the thoughts and emotions of those who have lived in the past and which now exist as a type of energy, a vast storehouse of knowledge and information, available to those who can tune in to it by psychic means.

Déjà vu is a French expression which means "already seen." It is the feeling of having been someplace before when you know you have never been there; of meeting someone new and feeling as if you have met them before; of knowing what someone is going to say just before they speak. Theories to explain this experience say that possibly there is a similarity between the two locations, the two people, the ongoing conversation. Other explanations are that these experiences are precognitive, or that the time dimensions of two worlds have somehow overlapped momentarily.

Divination is the practice of acquiring hidden knowledge through the supernatural, such as the oracle at Delphi, where the prophet went into a trance and uttered divine messages, supposedly directly from the gods of ancient Greece.

Dowsing is an age-old art used to locate not only water but other submerged items, including people, using a forked stick or a bent rod. Prehistoric rock paintings in Algeria show dowsers at work, and the ancient Chinese and Egyptians may also have practiced dowsing. Dowsing is still widely practiced today, particularly for locating wells, and it is documented that it works. A physical explanation is that the unseen water, minerals or other object under the earth emits a force, such as the electromagnetic fields that are often transmitted through water and that is then transmitted to the stick or divining rod and felt by the hands of the sensitive dowser as he walks through the fields. Map dowsing however also appears to be successful and cannot be explained in the same way, with felt vibrations or emissions directly from the earth. The dowser who accepts a psychic explanation thinks that all objects project an energy field, such as the aura, which some claim to be able to see around the head of others, and this energy field is felt by those sensitive to its vibrations. Dowsing is said to be used to find anything, including richly valuable oil fields or diamond lodes.

Uri Geller, the famed psychic, claims to have pinpointed a major coal deposit for South Africa's Anglo-Transvaal mining company by map dowsing, and claims that major oil companies have used him as an "airborne divining rod."

ESP or extrasensory perception is the ability to access information beyond the five known senses by using the sixth sense of intuition.

I Ching In China during the Shang dynasty, divination was done by inscribing symbols on the bottom shells of tortoises and then heating them. A message was found by reading the pattern of the cracks formed across the inscription after the heat was applied. During the Chou dynasty a traditional pattern of lines was established and judgments written that explained their significance. In the time of Confucius, additional texts, the Wings, were added. The result is the text known as the *I Ching* (the Book of Changes). The cosmological principles behind the *I Ching* is that of change, in the movement between the cosmic forces of yin and yang as represented by the divided and undivided lines of the traditional patterns. The resulting sixty-four patterns, called hexagrams, represent all possible situations or changes in creation. Examination of the hexagrams will furnish a description of the universe at that particular moment in its endless process of change and provide hints of its future course.

Kirlian photography has produced images that resemble what many psychics say they see when they observe someone's aura. During the photographic process, unexposed film is placed on an electrode, the object is placed on or near the film, and the electrode is subjected to high-voltage pulses. The film is developed and various kinds of halos or auras are seen to surround the object. The theory is that the film records the subtle energy field that surrounds all forms of life, as well as inanimate objects, energy that is not detectable by ordinary means. Kirlian photography can be affected by a number of physical factors such as temperature, moisture, the local micro environment, and pressure.

Other researchers have photographed the corona discharge patterns of human fingertips. As diagnostic tools the photos are said to reveal the presence of cancer, cystic fibrosis and other diseases in the body of the individual whose fingers were photographed.

Skeptics maintain that aura photography is only the result of moisture from the object touching the photographic plate. However, Keith Wagner, a researcher at California State University, performed some experiments in which he placed a lucite block as a moisture barrier between the object and the photographic plate, and still produced a Kirlian aura photograph.

Metaphysics is the branch of philosophy which uses a method of inquiry based on reason alone. In the twentieth century, the validity of metaphysical thinking has been disputed by those who assert that things which cannot be tested empirically have no meaning.

OBE, or out-of-body experience, is thought to be the breaking of the bonds of the physical world, allowing the spirit to travel beyond the body for a short time and then return.

Charles Lindbergh is said to have experienced such travel during the twenty-second hour of his 1927 transatlantic flight from New York to Paris. The plane was enclosed in a dense fog and Lindbergh stared at the instrument panel and fought off the desire to sleep. "I existed independent of time and matter," he recalled nearly fifty years later. "I felt myself departing from my body . . . emanating into the cockpit, extending through the fuselage as though no frame or fabric walls were there, angling upward, outward, until I reformed in an awareness far distant from the human form I left. But I remained connected to my body through a long-extended strand, a strand so tenuous that it could have been severed by a breath."

In *Journeys Out of the Body,* businessman Robert Monroe wrote a first-person account of his astral travels to other dimensions, including detailed statistical analyses of every detail of every known physical condition at the time of his OBEs. Monroe claims that anyone can travel outside the body with a little practice.

If you wish to try:

- In a dark warm room, lie down after loosening your clothing and removing all jewelry.
- Close your eyes, breathe deeply and regularly, and relax.
- Focus on a single image, such as an open doorway, as you drift into sleep. As you reach that state between wakefulness and sleeping, deepen your relaxation and concentrate on the dark just beyond your eyes.
- Because it is reported that there are actual physical vibrations that precede an OBE, imagine vibrations occurring in the room outside you and bring them down into your head.
- Guide them through your body until you can control the vibrations.
- Now concentrate on floating upward. You will feel your astral form rise from the bed.
- To return, focus on rejoining your astral and physical self.

Researchers have maintained that OBEs are a form of lucid dreaming in which the dreamer realizes that a dream is in progress. Anthropologist Dean Shells, who studied OBEs in sixty-seven different cultures, states that sleep is involved in about 80 percent of them.

Psychiatrist Glen Gabbard speculates that OBEs may be hypnagogic images—images that occur during the time one hovers between wakefulness and sleep. He concludes that such images are experienced as extremely real, thus causing them to be confused with actual OBEs.

Occultism means "to hide" and it is the belief in the validity of a variety of practices based on hidden knowledge about the universe and its mysterious forces. These forces can be contacted through various practices such as magic, alchemy or astrology. Occultism may also include a belief in beings, such as angels, deities, or spirits, who can be contacted by those who possess the knowledge of the appropriate rituals or spells and have special abilities for their use. There have been occult practices within nearly all civilizations. Western occultism has its roots in ancient Babylonian and Egyptian lore, especially as recorded and transmitted through neoplatonism and the Hermetic works, books and theories about the occult sciences. Augmented by Jewish mysticism, occultism was an obscure but important presence in the European Middle Ages (4th to 15th centuries). Medieval occult practice included astrology, alchemy and ceremonial magic rites for evoking spiritual beings. The renowned thirteenth-century Italian theologian Saint Thomas Aquinas believed in the effectiveness of alchemy and other occult arts.

Oneiromancy is divination from dreams.

Palmistry, also known as chiromancy, is the art of foretelling the future through the study of the palm of the hand. It was known among the Assyrians, Egyptians and Hebrews and recognized by philosophers such as Plato and Aristotle. Palmistry is chiefly concerned with the mounts of the palm, the lines on the mounts, and the lines interlacing the palm. The left hand supposedly reflects inbred characteristics and the right hand, acquired characteristics. Whether the opposite is true for those whose left hand is dominant is open to interpretation. Many ancient cultures considered left-handedness evil, and punished children who persisted in the use of their left hand for major tasks. Today's palmists have differing opinions on whether left-handedness makes a difference in reading the palm.

Each mount signifies a certain personality trait. The lines on the mounts relate to intelligence, love and personal fortune and are modified or corroborated by their positions in relationship to the other mounts and other lines.

Paranormal includes all those things which are beyond explanation by known scientific laws and can include subjects as far ranging as flying saucers and ghosts to telepathy and spiritualism.

Parapsychology is a branch of psychology which attempts, through scientific methodology, to explain and duplicate experiments with such things as telepathy and ESP.

Poltergeist comes from the German *poltern,* meaning to make noise, and *geist,* meaning ghost or spirit. It is the manifestation of psychokenisis, in which objects fly around the room, lights turn on or off by themselves, pictures fly off the walls. Reports of poltergeists appear to share one basic similarity: they concentrate on boys and girls just reaching puberty, a time of extreme physical and emotional stress. Many researchers into the phenomenon maintain that this is a product of the psychic energy of human emotions (usually that of teenagers), and not ghosts at all, but a kind of an extension of the energy of one individual. This phenomenon appears to confirm the existence of psychokenesis.

William G. Roll, project director of the Psychical Research Foundation and a leading poltergeist expert, evaluated 116 poltergeist cases and found that ninty-two of them focused on a particular family member, often a teenager between the ages of thirteen and fourteen years old.

Author and poltergeist-believer David Knight writes, "Often such boys and girls are undergoing deep-seated emotional stress in connection with developing sexual energies." Many investigators think this inner stress may in some unknown manner transfer its energy outside the body, causing the poltergeist manifestations.

There have been a number of case studies written, some in the form of haunted-house fiction, which recount the mysterious goings-on in some households. These strange occurrences usually are like a fever which eventually runs its course, then stops, often when the teenager involved passes through the pubertal crisis.

Precognition is the psychic phenomenon of being knowledgeable about events that have not yet occurred, foretelling the future.

Psi is word coined to use in place of the longer term extrasensory perception or intuition, and often includes everything being discussed which is considered paranormal.

Psychic means the ability to use extrasensory perception and connect with energy that cannot be explained by known scientific means.

Psychokenesis is the ability to affect objects at a distance by means other than known physical forces, such as levitating tables or causing paintings to fall off a wall.

Psychometry is the ability to discern information about an individual through possessions such as jewelry, photographs or clothing. There are a number of cultures that believe that when you take a photograph of an individual you capture that person's soul. For that reason a number of religious groups, including the Amish, refuse to have their photo taken. Many psychics claim they can view a photograph of someone and provide detailed and sometimes hidden information about the individual because their energy has been captured on the film.

The concept is based on the idea that the part includes the whole, similar to a hologram.

Scrying is using a crystal ball to see into the future or the past. The crystal ball gazer looks into the ball in a darkened room. Underneath the crystal is a mat or a dark cloth which prevents reflections from the outside from interfering. The diviner "reads" the mists and optical effects which appear. Frequently the crystal gazer will ask a question that can be answered with a yes or no. A mist that rises up in the globe is a "yes" response to the question, one that drifts downward is a "no." The use of a crystal ball is possibly based on the fact that in addition to being a clear globe, quartz crystals have long been recognized as having the ability to receive electrical signals, e.g. quartz watches and quartz radio receivers.

Spiritualism or necromancy, is the art of conjuring up revelations from the souls or spirits of the dead.

Synchronicity is a term coined by psychologist Carl Jung for the phenomenon of meaningful coincidences. He stated that synchronicity suggests that there can be a meaningful interconnection of casually unrelated events.

Tarot or cartomancy. The origins of the tarot are obscure. The symbols on the cards have been linked to Egyptian hieroglyphics. The word "hieroglyph" means a symbol or picture meant to represent a sound or a concept. The hieroglyph, after originating on the banks of the Nile, was eventually exported to the West by way of

Greece. Here the tarot was used mainly for fortune-telling. The tarot went through a number of changes as it was interpreted and reinterpreted by various scholars and artists. In the middle of the nineteenth century, a French philosopher and artist, Alphonse Constant, wrote a book about magic which included an interpretation of the symbolism of the cards. These cards eventually became accessible to many as they began to appear in print. The cards have evolved over the years, with many artists drawing creative and inspiring images for the cards. In the nineteenth century, artist Pamela Coleman-Smith made powerful drawings for what has become the most well-known deck—the Rider-Waite tarot.

Users of these cards believe that the tarot symbols form an unconscious link between man and the unknown, with each card representing an aspect of that relationship. As the subject turns over the cards, the relationship of each card to each other and to the subject creates a picture about life, the past, the present and the future. This unfolding picture is unique to the subject because it is the subject's hand that shuffles, and selects each card. The cards, as they are laid out and turned up, become a mirror of the individual, reflecting self-realization or self-illusion.

Angel cards and fairy cards have recently become popular because, unlike the tarot, they have a word or phrase on them which can be interpreted by the individual using them. A tarotologist or reader is not needed, because such cards don't require understanding the complex symbolism and linkage necessary with the tarot. For example, an angel card, which is randomly drawn, might have the word "flexibility" on it. The reader, by participating in the selection of a card, can then decide that the selection was not random but was drawn for them by some unseen force. The word on the card can be seen as specific to their needs at that time and they can apply the phrase or word they have drawn to anything in their life they wish. In this case, they can apply the "flexibility" concept to any area in which they might think they need to be less rigid.

Telepathy is the ability to transfer thought through time and space from one individual's mind to another, often instantaneously.

Expanded Consciousness or Mysticism

For centuries there have been reports of mystics, Zen masters, Sufis, yogis and shamans who were telepathic, clairvoyant, able to levitate, survive when buried alive, able to walk on burning coals and perform all kinds of miraculous feats. True or not, exaggerations or not, they all point the way to the very human need for states of consciousness that are beyond the ordinary, states that link the individual to some kind of energy apart from everyday reality.

Because the ability to access psychic phenomena has, until now, been unexplainable by any kind of explicit scientific model, it has been believed that there must be either a mystical, spiritual or occult explanation for it. For many people, anything unexplained is unacceptable and frightening. Those who believed that to accept psychic phenomena meant that it was also necessary to believe in angels, messages from the dead, or to accept the reality of other spooky, mysterious and occult experiences, usually scrupulously avoided the topic, laughed about it, or looked with scorn at anyone who expressed an interest.

For centuries, oracles, shamans and seers have accepted these wonders as being real through expanded consciousness, although they never spoke of magnetic or electrical fields, energy fields, or various forms of light. But it now appears that these mystics, if they were to meet with today's sophisticated scientists, might have a meeting of the minds. They would surely all agree that the Newtonian view of the world as consisting of solid objects is obsolete. They might believe that there may be theories of quantum physics or experiential meta-physics which can provide a plausible explanation of a universal energy, in the form of force fields, that can instantaneously be accessible.

If we accept the concept that the universe is interconnected through energy fields that transcend time and space, there is no need to hobble the concept with mysticism and occultism. We can simply accept and understand that psychic phenomena are part of everyday life we have just forgotten how to use.

FIVE

Focusing, Visualizing and Meditation: Why Do We Need Any of That Stuff?

Close up his eyes and draw the curtain close;
And let us all to meditation
　　　—William Shakespeare, *King Henry VI*

A s a child you possessed psychic skills. All you are doing now is recapturing them.

If you have been practicing visualization—using your imagination to see something in your mind's eye and focusing, paying attention to small details—you have probably noticed an increase in the number of coincidences, or synchronicities, occurring in your life.

Many people dismiss coincidences, but they are often the first clue that you have made a psychic connection. Pay attention: every connection you make prepares you to be psychic once again—not just for the moment, but as a way of life. You are setting the stage for knowing in a very different way.

Our emphasis here is on learning how to increase the ability to make contact with that energy we call psychic power, our sixth sense, so that we can do it easily and regularly. Psychic events occur when you are *relaxed,* both physically and mentally; visualization works best when you are feeling at ease. When the unconscious mind is at its most powerful, you are producing more and more *alpha* and in a trance state, *theta* brain waves, so psychic messages in the form of visual images can break through, making a deeper and stronger impact. To connect to your sixth sense easily, relax and visualize.

Relaxing

Understanding that relaxing is important is often easier than doing it. Exercises will help relieve tense muscles but sometimes it takes effort to break long held habits.

When you come home at the end of your day, it is easy to kick off your shoes and drop into your most comfortable chair with a drink in your hand and turn on the TV.

Don't.

Instead, remember that conscious diaphragmatic breathing is more important in bringing about a state of relaxation than anything else you can do quickly.

Imagine, in the safety of your own home, that you are inhaling the energy of the universe, gathering its power and strength into you. If you have some music which you are particularly fond of, something that is relaxing instead of stimulating, put it on when you come home. *River of Life* by kurt van sickle might be an excellent choice, or any other soft, soothing and healing sounds that promote the balance of your mind and body. Go ahead and kick off your shoes, and with your bare feet in contact with the ground, for just five minutes, move to the music: breathing, reaching, breathing, stretching, breathing, dancing. Not only will this make dealing with the kids, dinner and whatever else you have to do less stressful, you will find that it is easier to relax at bedtime as you prepare yourself for the psychic visions that your dreams are going to bring.

Progressive Relaxation

Sit in a comfortable position. Loosen any restrictive clothing. Beginning with the feet, tighten the muscles completely and hold for a brief count of five—and then suddenly let go. Do not hold your breath, but breathe in completely while tensing and breathe out when you let your muscles relax. Move up through the muscles of the body, up to and including the facial muscles, tensing and relaxing. Finally, tense all the muscles in your body and take in a deep breath. Hold that tension for a count of five; now relax, and during a slow count of five, exhale slowly. You should feel relaxed all over, because it is the contrast between tension and relaxation which generates deeper relaxation than other exercises and speeds up the experience, while increasing your awareness of what being relaxed feels like. Once you have relaxed, your subconscious is more open to access the energy of the universe.

Quoting his well-known psychic wife Mary Craig Sinclair, novelist Upton Sinclair wrote in *Mental Radio,* in which he recorded experiments they conducted together where she was able to reproduce drawings made by others in rooms miles away: "The first thing you must do is learn to have undivided attention, or concentration. Put your attention on one subject, such as joy, or peace, and hold it there as steadily as you can. At the same time, you must relax, because it is concentration with relaxation that creates the ESP-favorable state."

Many psychics say that they can readily go in and out of trances, and it is in this state that they access their sixth sense. Shirley MacLaine's book *Out on a Limb* is a popular work in which she introduced the general reading audience to trance channelers. A televised version of her book showed two individuals reenacting a trance state. The dictionary definition of a trance is a state of profound mental distraction in which a person is less aware of normal external realities—in other words—self-hypnosis or meditation.

The *Titanic*

The Reverend Charles Morgan, the minister of Winnipeg's Rosedale Methodist Church in Canada, often lay down for a few minutes before beginning services in order to ask for and receive guidance and direction for his Sunday sermon. According to a report in the *Journal of the American Society for Psychical Research,* Rev. Morgan drifted off into a semi-sleeping state, actually a trance, on the morning of Sunday, April 14, 1912. As he lay in his study, he heard many people calling for help above the roar of the water, as if they were drowning in a pounding surf. Above this terrifying noise, he heard the music of an old hymn, often sung for the protection of sailors. "O hear us when we cry to Thee / For those in peril on the sea." Stunned, Morgan could not understand the experience but he knew it was more than a dream, it was very real. He was filled with apprehension and by the time of the Sunday service, the experience had unnerved him so drastically that he told his congregation about his experience. He didn't know if it had any meaning, but he asked them to join in singing the hymn he had heard.

The whole world was shocked when they read the next morning of the sinking of the supposedly unsinkable *Titanic* on her maiden voyage. Later, survivors would say that only two hours earlier, before the great vessel hit the iceberg that tore a huge hole in her hull, the ship's chaplain had led them in singing the hymn that Rev. Morgan had heard in his apparently prophetic dream. The minister and his congregation could only hope that their joining in the song may have helped ease the passage to the next world of the drowning victims as they sank beneath the waves.

Rev. Morgan did not know anyone on the *Titanic*. But it is not unusual that when the energy of many individuals is concentrated, those who are sensitive will connect with the occurrence.

Trance

J. Z. Knight claims that she uses a trance state to access her 35,000-year-old spirit guide. When she awakens from the trance, she has no knowledge of what happened. She must rely on others to tell her what she said and how she behaved

The trance state is brought about by a variety of methods. When self-induced, it usually can be done by trained muscle relaxation, eye fixation and concentrating on one's own breathing. Similar to a brief meditation, it is a state of consciousness wholly dissimilar to either wakefulness or sleep. During it, attention is withdrawn from the outside world and is concentrated on mental, sensory and physiological experiences. With practice, you can learn to enter a trance state easily, readily, within moments and still be safe in your surroundings.

Ideally, you want to be able to access your psychic powers at any time, not just after you have relaxed and have meditated in the quiet of your home. You want to be able to access your sixth sense when you are in the middle of a busy intersection, at a crowded restaurant, in a heavily traveled shopping mall. In order to be able to do this you must practice being relaxed. Edgar Cayce said that he could easily put himself into this state at any time he chose, whenever he wanted. With practice, you can too.

Mae and the Images

Mae encouraged everyone to explore their psychic self, to develop their own abilities. She listened to many tales of paranormal experiences. "Sometimes," she would say, "I feel like a doctor at a cocktail party. I have to listen to everybody's story of the mysterious experience they have had happen to them." Of course, it was easy for people to reveal their psychic experiences, to tell of their predictive dreams that had come true or déjà vu events when they were absolutely sure what was going to happen next. They were talking to someone who believed in the paranormal and valued the psychic domain. She helped many explore their psychic potential and motivated them to examine the world of power that opened to them through their own intuition.

When people asked what it felt like to experience that sixth sense and what they might do with it, she told them, "Once you have relaxed and centered yourself with a few deep breaths, silently ask a question in a simple form. It doesn't matter what it is that you want an answer about, it could be something life-altering or simply a color choice for painting a room. Send out a psychic signal and wait for a response. That reply might be an image, a picture in your mind, a voice in your head, a sense of suddenly knowing that something you were ambivalent about is no longer undecided. The exact form the answer comes in doesn't matter. What is important is that you learn to recognize the answer that has suddenly come to you. You are positive, then, that the answer you get is right for you. Once you are relaxed and centered, just ask your question and wait to see what happens."

Liberation—Psychic Guidance

Now that you are relaxed and focused—be psychic!

If you have depended on others to tell you what to do, if you have relied on religious leaders, friends, family, or even strangers such as tarot readers or astrologers to advise you when you have been hesitant or unsure about decisions in your life, accessing your own sixth sense can be very liberating. Now, you will make these decisions for yourself. You will learn to ask for direction and then listen to the guidance that comes, to make your own choices with help from a beneficent universe, not from others who may or may not have your best interests at heart.

Dreaming

Dreams have always been associated with telepathy and foretelling the future. Research by psychiatrist Montague Ullman, psychologist Stan Krippner and collaborators at the Maimonides Medical Center in New York has shown that the dream state is favorable for accessing psychic information.

The nature of dreams has been explored in many clinical and laboratory studies. These studies show that dreams are more perceptual than conceptual: Things are seen and heard rather than being subjected to thought. Visual experience is present in almost all dreams; auditory experience in some 50 percent; and touch, taste, smell and pain in a relatively small percentage. The work of American sleep researchers Eugene Aserinsky and Nathaniel Kleitman has shown that dreaming takes place during a biologically unique state. Their work showed that REM-sleep (rapid-eye-movement sleep), occurs cyclically during sleep and is characterized by activation of the autonomic nervous system. This REM-sleep occurs at intervals of about 90 minutes and altogether it constitutes about 25 percent of the night's sleep. Their evidence indicates that a dream period lasts from five to twenty minutes.

Since dream material seems to fade from consciousness as soon as we awaken, it makes sense to try to capture these images as soon as possible so that we can attempt to discover what their symbols mean.

Psychic Dreamers

Margaret Mitchell, author of *Gone With the Wind,* said that she dreamed most of the characters and events. When she awoke she simply transferred the images to paper. Robert Louis Stevenson, who wrote *Treasure Island* and *The Strange Case of Dr. Jekyll and Mr. Hyde,* reported that he wrote his famous works in a dreamlike trance state. His characters paraded before his eyes, speaking and acting out their drama as he watched.

Thomas Edison had tried thousands of different substances looking for the right material to make the filament for the electric light bulb. He had tried platinum, carbonized paper, bamboo thread—but everything he tried either wasn't bright enough, or burned up in too brief a time. In a dream, the solution came to him: A loop of cotton thread impregnated with lamp black and then baked in a carbonizing oven. Although it sounds complicated, it wasn't to the inventor, who had spent hours and hours trying to find the right substance. He knew that he had found something that would burn for perhaps 100 hours and at relatively little expense. He immediately knew when he woke up that he had his answer.

The list of people who have found life-altering and enhancing answers to their problems through dreams is endless. General George S. Patton Jr., made battle plans; Dr. Frederick Banting solved the problem of diabetes; Elias Howe perfected the lock-stitch sewing machine; Civil War slave Harriet Tubman found safe passage for hundreds of people in her underground railroad; golfer Jack Nicklaus solved his bad grip woes; and the surreal scenes in the films of Federick Fellini were envisioned in his dreams.

You, too, can become a psychic dreamer.

Dream Symbolism

Psychic dreams can offer guidance—send messages that need to be heard, speak the truth or bring a personal message, once you interpret the symbolism present in them. They can alert you to dangers that you have chosen to ignore or didn't see.

However, the symbolism of your dreams is often couched in the language of your subconscious. Your dreams may only represent fragments of ideas and they often require some work on your part to understand their meaning. Look around at your world and see what clothes, furniture, decorative accessories, pictures on the walls and all your possessions tell you about the things *you* think are important—because the psychic domain will use them to talk to you through your dreams.

If you have trouble understanding a symbol in your dream, try free association or ask yourself how the image makes you feel. Because we have all been taught to control our emotions most of the time, it may take some time to allow the meaning of your symbolism to become clear. With practice you will find that your understanding of your symbology will grow rapidly, bringing you pleasure as you interpret your dreams to your benefit.

In your dreams you can find people who will inspire you and help you to grow. You can spend time with people you have never met who can give you wise counsel and healing information. Sleeping and dreaming can make you look forward to the answers a night's sleep might bring.

Hillary Clinton and Eleanor Roosevelt

In 1996 the press encouraged us to laugh at First Lady Hillary Clinton because she revealed she had "talked" with Eleanor Roosevelt while writing her book *It Takes a Village*. The press labeled her as odd for contacting the dead but it is doubtful that Mrs. Clinton expected a reply. She wasn't entering into spiritualism, she was using a well-known visualization technique to stimulate her imagination. Under the guidance of Jean Houston, an academic and one of the founders of the Foundation for Mind Research, which studies ways to help people think more creatively, Mrs. Clinton spent ten days exploring a classic role-playing game.

It is not unusual for those who connect psychically with some of the great minds of the past to suddenly find inspiration and excellent ideas for their work. Perhaps Mrs. Clinton ought to thank Mrs. Roosevelt for the fact that her book became a bestseller.

Your Dream Work

For the next thirty days:

1. Tell yourself, just before going to sleep, that you *are* going to dream and you *will* remember that dream. Studies have shown that such self-programming can be effective if done consistently.

2. Program yourself to focus on questions you want answered, desires you want fulfilled. For example:

As for psychic guidance:

Give me a vision of an invention that will make me rich and famous.

Show me the person I will marry.

Provide psychic guidance so that I can become a _____.

Reveal the solution to my problem, which is _____.

Reveal the answer to the question I have about _____.

What is the truth about _____ *memory I have.*

Write your request in your dream journal just before you go to sleep. Keep it nearby. Be specific. If you ask an imprecise question, you are likely to get an imprecise and unsatisfactory answer.

3. Before you are fully awake, lie still for a while, search for the images from your dreams. Allow them to flow before you move around and stretch or make getting-up movements, as that will chase the dream fragments away. Write down or record key words from your dream, include as many fragments as you can. This will make it easier to write the dream up in more detail, before it is gone from your memory.

If you don't get an answer to your question right away, repeat your question each night. An answer will come.

4. Keep a dream journal. By committing yourself to journaling you are committing yourself to dreaming. You may recall only a fragment, a shape, an image, an impression, a mood or

a feeling. As you keep your journal you will dream more frequently, and you will remember more details from your dreams. The only way to determine if your dreams are precognitive is to record them and then review them. Set aside a space in your journal to record the times your dreams were accurate.

5. Identify your dream symbols. As Jung said, no one can interpret dream symbols except the dreamer. Pay attention to details. Do not dismiss any connection between your dream and events which come to pass. Compare the events of the day with your dreams, events which take place both before *before and after* your dream. Sometimes you may want something very badly and find that your wishes are fulfilled in your dreams. But don't be misled by subconscious desires; they will provide fantasy-fulfilling dreams. You can tell the difference because the psychic dream will have a clarity, detail, authenticity and emotion that the wish-fulfillment dream doesn't. Pay attention to dreams to which you have a physical response when you think about them—a chill, a quickening of your heart or a sudden intake of breath. Now it is up to you to see what you can learn from the psychic realm.

6. At the end of a month, analyze your dream diary. Look for patterns or recurring symbolism.

Dream Interpretation

The Australian aborigines have worked with guidance dreams for more than fifty thousand years. Using sand, pigment, and blood they create designs that, to the untutored western eye, look like highly contemporary abstract paintings but are actually mythic landscapes. In their vision of life, time has two dimensions: reality and a spiritual conception of reality. These people take their dreams just as seriously as physical reality, as do Native Americans and many other cultures. In some cultures it is believed that the dream world is more important than the physical world. People depend on the shaman, someone who has perhaps spent an entire lifetime pursuing an expanded consciousness, who is both healer and leader, to listen to their dream experiences, examine the drawings of these mythical landscapes and representational paintings, and help interpret them. The shaman is expected to aid them in applying the knowledge gained while sleeping to develop maps for their daily lives. While some may consider these cultures primitive or unsophisticated, they may be more in tune with the natural world and the universe around them than we are, reaping a fullness of living that might in some ways be more complete than our own.

In the West we have lost the art of dream interpretation, just as we have lost the ability to connect with our sixth sense, the world of the paranormal. Often it is only the psychiatrist who helps today's dreamers deal with their dream life. By recording dreams and evaluating the recurrent themes or the symbols that appear in our sleep, we can come to understand their meaning and perhaps connect more fully with the universe. By reconnecting with dreaming you are on the way to reconnecting to your psychic self.

Precognitive dreams are often extremely vivid with a considerable amount of emotion and they are often about someone to whom you are emotionally connected: a husband, wife, lover, parent or child. At the same time, you may find that deaths, disasters and traumatic events that have absolutely nothing to do with you—or which you are helpless to prevent or delay—are the easiest kinds of precognitive events to pick up. Crises send a stronger signal and negative predictions are often the kinds that new psychics get. You have been acting as a psychic receiver and have picked up something from the collective unconscious, the universal mind. You should not feel any responsibility if the dream is about something such as a plane crash or other disaster, something which you cannot prevent or warn others about. Such occurrences can be enough to deter anyone from the path to psychic enlightenment. It may be disconcerting to be privy to information you don't want to know, to events you can't alter. But remember, the purpose of fostering this talent is to know ourselves and our world, to be responsive to the universe. These dreams are evidence of the connection to the psychic world around you and should reinforce your belief in your ability to link with the energy that is out there. Dreaming will allow you to connect with others more completely and to join with the forces of the universe in ways you have forgotten.

You may find that in a dream you are given the answer to a question that will send you on a path entirely different from the one you were planning to take. These dreams don't mean that there is nothing you can do; dreams only present possibilities. The ultimate responsibility about what you do after you interpret your dreams is yours. Sometimes a dream will send a message about some kind of danger; when that occurs you should definitely pay close attention because you have been given a protection. You can take precautions; sometimes you will be forewarned about a health condition before any physical signs manifest themselves. Always remember that in intuitive states, when we connect with the collective unconscious, the structure of time is different. Past, present, and future are not as they are in everyday reality, so you need to examine the dream carefully to see if it might relate to something that has already happened, something there is no longer any need to worry about.

Your Psychic Focus

Different people will have differing psychic focuses: You will learn what is right for you and discover your personal route to the paranormal. Perhaps it is aura reading, or dream interpretation, or telepathy. As you learn more about your psychic self, you will find the direction that is right for you. The more you experiment with differing psychic modes, the more you will become aware of the energies that can be transmitted from the universe and others to you, and from you to others. You will realize that the physical boundaries you have always thought existed are just mental barriers that can be overcome. As these physical barriers fall away and you access one form of psychic experience, you will find that as it develops, others may begin to appear.

It is thought that the continuous energy the human body emits is held by any object they have handled. If they have had an emotional connection to that object, then the energy is even stronger. This energy is often used to stay connected to a loved one or a place through a keepsake, a pressed flower, a special stone, or a photo.

It is thought that events involving very strong emotions, can leave that energy in either a place or an object. Most religions recognize this phenomenon. People may carry an image, a medallion, a talisman or amulet with energy intended for a particular purpose—protection against sickness or to bring a particular kind of assistance. The ancient Egyptians wore charms, as did the Greeks. Jews place a slip of parchment inscribed with passages of the Talmudic law at the front door of their homes. Early Christians wore a charm with the Greek word *abraxas* engraved on it because the word was thought to have mystic value.

If you have ever taken an object from someone's hand and been overwhelmed with the emotion you suddenly felt, you may be a person whose connection to the paranormal is through psychometry, a concept explained by the idea of a holographic universe, where an object can hold the energy, the essence of an individual. The object can then be used to represent the whole.

The energy field of any individual is experienced by all of us. If you have ever liked or disliked someone the instant you are introduced to them, if you have known the mood of a stranger without even speaking to them, if you have sensed from a friend's voice on the telephone that something is wrong, even though they are talking only in generalities, then you have experienced that person psychometrically. If you find that you are energized by someone, you might want to take a good look at that individual, because this could be an important energy connection for you. If another individual makes you feel drained, think what this relationship could be: It may be negativity that you want to avoid.

Or you might be a healer, one who can help others through

the laying on of hands, a very special form of therapeutic work. Do you often readily put your hand on the shoulder of someone who is upset or in need of comfort? Do you easily pat and stroke your loved ones, your children and pets? Have you sat at the bedside of someone who is ill and held their hand? If you have a headache or a stomach ache, do you find that you put your hand there to make yourself feel better? You are intuitively using a form of psychometry, transmitting energy through your hands.

Stephanie and the Energy Vampire

Stephanie worked in a small office where the boss, Dave, was known by the nickname Gloomy Gus. Another employee, Anne, the file clerk, usually got the worst of it. Her desk abutted Dave's, she tried to avoid looking in his direction, fearful of his attention being focused on her and what she was doing.

Everyone was afraid of him. He always appeared to be in a foul mood, sullen and silent. When he did speak, it was to bark at the others, giving orders and complaining that nothing they did pleased him.

Anne frequently hid in the file room, pretending her work there was taking longer than was really necessary, staying as far away from Dave as she could get. "He just puts such a damper on the room, you can feel the bad vibes when he comes through the door," she complained.

Stephanie and Anne would go out to lunch together and complain about the negative energy Dave gave off. Some days it seemed to permeate the very air of the office.

Anne said, "I just hate being around him. It's like a dark cloud follows him all the time. Just thinking about him makes me feel sick."

Occasionally Stephanie talked to Mae about Dave and how everyone who worked with him disliked being in the same room with the man.

Mae said, "You better pay attention, Stephanie. A person with that much negative energy can really drain you. Have you thought of finding another job?"

Stephanie had a long list of reasons why she had to stay in that job and how it was useless to complain about him because management "wouldn't do anything about Dave because he is efficient and a dedicated company man."

At Mae's urging, Stephanie began to put up a protective psychic shield against Dave. But when she told Anne to do the same thing, Anne laughed. "Oh, Stephanie, that's just nonsense. I couldn't do that, it sounds like black magic."

Months later, when Anne had to have surgery for cancer, Stephanie thought that Dave's negativity had a lot to do with Anne's illness and that she should have been protecting herself against all that energy draining. She exclaimed, "That Dave, he's an energy vampire!"

Of course, no one can say Anne's cancer was caused by Dave's negative energy but his negativity put a tremendous amount of stress on everyone, and constant stress has been proven to lower the body's immune system.

We can be like sponges, absorbing the energy from the sea of energy that surrounds us. Energy from others can be both experienced and exchanged. When your own energy is low you can be vulnerable to the energy of others around you, so it is a good idea to be extremely aware of the kind of energy put out by the people you spend time with. If individuals are emitting good positive energy they can be uplifting and beneficial, but you also need to be on the lookout for negative energy so that it does not do any damage of any kind.

Psychometry

Think about psychometry the next time you are introduced to a stranger and you shake their hand for the first time. That hand may be cold, warm, damp, dry, firm, flabby. What do you feel in your own body from that handshake? Repulsed, attracted? Is this individual strong, unwell, anxious to leave, sincere, happy, entertaining, depressed? Your impressions on the first touch may give you more information than a twenty minute casual conversation.

Recall the theory of Bohm: we are in an vast ocean of energy, a universe crossed by electromagnetic force fields; things are not solid but are waves of energy, moving, and interconnecting. Or recall Bentov's theory that everything in the universe is oscillating. There are important implications for the psychic ability known as psychometry.

If you think you might want to experience the capacity to hold a physical object and receive specific information about people, places or events to which the object is related, try the following experiment with the very next letter you receive in the mail.

- Before opening it, rub your hands together briskly to increase their sensitivity and arouse the minor chakras in your hands and fingertips. (We have all seen old movies where the safecracker rubs his hands together before he tries to feel the clicks on the dial of the combination lock. Although he probably knew nothing about chakras, he understood he could increase the sensitivity of his fingertips by doing this.)
- Examine the envelope closely, turning it over. Then close your eyes, take a deep breath, relax your tongue and hold the letter with both hands. Feel it thoroughly, the texture of the paper, its weight. Place it against your abdomen where your solar plexus, or third chakra, is located, or against your forehead where your third eye, brow or sixth chakra is located.
- Ask yourself whether or not it contains good news.
- Try to get a feeling of the mood of the person who wrote it.
- Feel your own emotions as you hold the letter.

- Ask some simple questions that can be answered with a "yes" or "no" about the sender.

At first, you may only get general impressions. You may feel a tingling, a change in your own body temperature or in the envelope in your hand. With practice you will find that you will improve in getting a feel for what is in the envelope before you open it.

Personal Psychometric Exercise

This is a fascinating experiment that you can do with another person.

- Hold an object belonging to the other person—keys, a ring, or watch. Feel all the surfaces with your fingertips and the palms of your hands.
- Close your eyes and relax, concentrating on the object you are holding.
- Describe the first thing that comes into your awareness, no matter how strange or unusual it might seem.
- As you continue to relax and concentrate, describe in detail the images that appear. Do not let your logical mind take over and analyze the images, instead let them flow.
- Stay aware of any smells, colors, or sounds that come with the images.
- When you are finished, verify the information you have received with the owner of the object.
- Then repeat the experiment in the reverse, with your experiment partner holding an object that belongs to you.

Psychometry for Therapeutic Touch

I have found my own contact with the energy of the universe through therapeutic touch. As a registered nurse and a psychologist,

I have been a facilitator for healing, beyond what one might expect. When interacting with someone in such a setting I consider myself no more than a catalyst or a conductor, so that the built-in healer that is already present in a sick or injured person can be stimulated by both my energy and the energy of the universe.

Therapeutic healing is a very specialized form of psychometry. The American Holistic Nurses' Association endorses weekend seminars given throughout the country and which are open to all those who are sincerely interested in the use of energy to support the healing of another. However, remember that in order for energy from you to be beneficial to another, you need to feel an empathy with that person. This higher level of energy and the legendary expression of this most ancient of the healing arts is only effective when done with a loving heart.

Our emotions and our thoughts alter our energy fields. So if we are negatively thinking, "This person has cancer, they cannot possibly get well," then no matter how thorough a ritual it appears to be, the energy generated may not be helpful at all. At the other end of this interaction, if the person receiving the healing touch is very negative, doubting that energy fields exist or that such an experience can be of help, they can put up a barrier to any helpful energy. It is most effective if both are in agreement that they will work together to strengthen the immune system, increase energy, or reduce pain.

There are many ancient stories of healers who simply touched strangers and the sufferer was instantly cured of deadly ailments. While you may believe this to be true, remember that we have laws now against diagnosing or treating others without proper credentials. However, if you have the acceptance of a loved one, perhaps a family member, you can, by "scanning" their body with your hands, find areas where there may be increased heat or coolness. By "sending" them some of your energy, you may be able to increase their vitality or relieve some pain. It is well documented that touch has a bonding and healing effect on both people and animals.

A number of nurses and dental hygienists have told me that sometimes, during their daily work, they simply emphatically send a message of affection and concerned compassion to the patient in their care.

Pet Psychometric Exercise

Animals are quite responsive to therapeutic or healing touch, as well as telepathy. It appears that they can feel energy changes and emotions from humans very quickly. If you have an animal who is not feeling well or one who is hyper, jumping up and annoying visitors, you might try the following.

- Touch the animal very lightly, using only a featherlike touch with the very ends of your fingertips. Touch the animal only around the head and ears while you talk softly in a calm and gentle voice. Feel love toward the creature, visualize healing and calming energy flowing from your fingers to the chakra at the crown of the animal's head. Send mental pictures of the behavior you desire, see the injury or sickness leaving your pet as you talk about helping a part of the animal kingdom to be well and serene.
- Take the animal on your lap. An excited or fearful animal will calm down if you handle it gently.
- Once the animal relaxes, with one hand an inch or so above the animal's fur or skin, make very slow gently stroking motions, beginning at the head and going all the way along the body, ending with the tip of the tail. Gently shake your hand, as if there is water on the end of your fingertips, dropping all that negative energy away from your pet. Try this without actually petting while you speak in soothing tones and watch what happens. You may find that you have relaxed and calmed your friend without actually touching.
- If this is effective, try gently petting the animal, slowly, softly

and only in the area around the head and the ears in the beginning. Speak softly, telling your pet how much love you feel and how rewarded you are to have him in your life.

- Try five minutes daily of this kind of therapeutic touching and soft talking. Within two weeks you may find that your pet is calmer, gentler, and much more cooperative.

Mona says that when she needs to take her cat to the vet, she only has to think about the cat carrier, and her cat Felix disappears under the bed.

Jerry says he no longer has to call his dog Lucky to be fed, he just has to think about dog food. Jerry doesn't think this is conditioning, as he not good about keeping to a regular feeding schedule. These pet lovers and many others have no doubt that they have established telepathic links with their four-footed friends.

Stranger Psychometric Exercise

The next time you interact with a stranger, such as a supermarket clerk or the person at the counter at the dry cleaners, try sending them some healing energy. It can be done mentally as you talk or as your hands touch when you pass them your money or take your change.

- Relax, be sure to relax your tongue, take a few deep breaths and think:
  "You are feeling well and strong." Feel your energy field reaching out toward the person. Or "You are calm and happy."
- Just before your hands touch, send energy down your arms to your fingers. Visualize healing color surrounding them. You may be surprised to see this stranger's shoulders lift, their head come up, and you often will be rewarded with

a beautiful smile. Who wouldn't want to have that kind of loving experience?

The Chakras—Energy Centers

Ancient Indian yogic literature contains information about special energy centers which are believed to exist within the body. Sanskrit writings refers to these energy centers as "chakras" which is translated to mean "wheels." They are said to resemble swirling whirlpools of energy. This energy travels along energy rivers known as *nadis* to the areas of the body each controls. Anatomically, each major chakra corresponds with a major nerve plexus and a major endocrine gland. There are seven major chakras and twenty-one minor chakras from the top of the head to the end of the spine. The major chakras are:

1. Root or Base—the base of the spine, near the end of the spine.
2. Sacral—lower abdomen, just below the navel.
3. Solar plexus—upper middle abdomen, tip of the breastbone.
4. Heart—directly over the heart.
5. Throat—near the Adam's apple, mid-throat.
6. Brow—mid forehead, slightly above the bridge of the nose.
7. Crown—the top of the head.

It is thought that the chakras translate energy of higher frequencies into a glandular/hormonal product which affects the entire body. These hormones are altered by thoughts and emotions. The alteration manifests itself outside the body in energy fields (auras) which can be seen.

Esoteric literature also suggests that the crown chakra takes in currents of energy and then distributes it down through the spinal cord to the lower charkas. The upper three chakras are thought to be associated with different types of psychic energy: the brow chakra with clairvoyance, the throat with clairaudience, the heart with clairsentience. The heart chakra is considered the transitional chakra, communicating between the higher spiritual energies of the upper three and the lower earthly energies of the remaining three. In literature it occupies a symbolically central position—between heaven and earth.

Meditation and Crystals

A common object for meditation focus can be a beautifully polished river stone, an ordinary rock from your own yard or a precious gem that has some meaning for you. Quartz crystals have often been used in meditation, not only because they are beautiful and are thought capable of focusing energy and have all kinds of beneficial effects, but perhaps because they exhibit what is known the piezoelectric effect; that is, they can act as receivers and are said to vibrate at a beneficial frequency. While a beautiful quartz crystal can be delightful to look at, it is not necessary to purchase an expensive one. Choose one that pleases you, perhaps seems to glow when hit by the light or feels warm in your hand.

Those who know something about early radios may recall that they were called crystal sets because quartz crystals were part of the receiver. Quartz is made of silicon dioxide and is chemically the same as sand. Silicon Valley in California has developed into the location of a multibillion dollar industry because silicon chips have important applications today in the electronics industry. But before manufacturers shifted to growing their own silicon crystals— which can be infused with precise amounts of other elements and can be controlled for electrical and thermal conductivity, optical activity and other factors—the industry began with quartz chips which responded in a great variety of ways to light, microwaves, gamma rays and electricity.

If you wish, try holding a small quartz crystal in your hand when you meditate or visualize. Place it on your desk while you work or under your pillow if you want to dream. It is said that they can increase your concentration and improve your performance on your job. Many psychics wear a crystal as a piece of jewelry or carry one in a pocket. You may find it to be a thought—energy amplifier. Some aspects of the human energy system are so similar that it is thought that humans are in harmony with natural quartz crystals. A quartz crystal held in the left hand should be neurologically connected to the right hemisphere of the brain.

Mineralogists classify crystals based on geometric patterns of their formations and some believe that their vibratory energy has a correspondence to the major chakras as follows:

Chakra	Crystal Classification	Mineral which Typifies
Crown	Triclinic	Turquoise
Brow	Monoclinic	Jade
Throat	Orthorhombic	Topaz
Heart	Tetragonal	Copper
Solar Plexus	Hexagonal	Emerald
Sacral	Cubic	Diamond
Root	Trigonal	Amethyst

If nothing more, you may find that focusing on a beautiful piece of one of the minerals of the earth will bring you into a more thoughtful harmony with the energies of nature.

Psychometric Self-Health Scanning

You are going to examine your own body and perform a healing exercise on yourself:

- Perform a brief meditation and focusing exercise, then relax

with loosened clothing in a comfortable place where you
will not be disturbed.

- With your eyes closed, visualize a tiny light entering the top
of your head through the crown chakra.

- Follow this tiny light as it travels throughout your body,
observing, feeling for differences in temperature—up and
down your arms and legs, and then into your internal organs.
Take your time.

- If you find any area of your body that seems weak or lacking
in vitality, or if you have a problem you are already aware of,
such as a weak back or a troublesome knee, make a note of
it and mentally send some healing and cleansing energy to
that spot. You may visualize that energy in any way you wish:
it is your energy and your body. Choose a color that seems
healing and soothing to you, or visualize the problem draining
out through your feet or your fingertips and then being
replaced with healthy strong tissue that your energy is creating.

Visualization or guided imagery is well documented to be beneficial. You can "represent" germs, bacteria, or viruses with whatever
symbolism works for you. Young cancer patients have zapped their
cancer cells by imagining their immune cells as tiny spaceships. Sailors
have imagined binding up sore knees with the rigging from a ship;
people with carpal tunnel syndrome have mentally sent roses to their
wrists so that the flowers' psychic essence can soothe the pain there.

The method you select to send your energy internally is only as
limited as your own imagination. It may be that you have problems
that chronically bother you, such as a tense and sore muscle in your
neck, or a spot on your lower back that is tender. Scan these areas
frequently and take care of them with your own psychic energy.

Many people have been surprised that by taking the time to do
this internal scanning, they have not only felt better and had less
pain, but they have uncovered a health problem of which they were
unaware and were able to see a doctor before it could become
more serious.

Sandi and a Psychic Scan

Sandi had a full-time job at a newspaper, a loving husband, several children and a big ranch house, plus two horses in a barn out back. She didn't have much time to think about herself or her health. When she became interested in therapeutic energy healing, she decided to practice self-scanning; it interested her, and she thought it would be a time saver. During her psychic scan Sandi felt a warmer than normal spot in her right breast. She went back and examined it carefully with her fingertips and she was sure she had found a lump. Frightened, she made an appointment with her doctor for an examination. Sandi's doctor didn't feel what she had felt, but he sent her for a mammogram. The night before that test Sandi had a dream. "I saw both my children crying at my bedside. I was sure the mammogram would turn up something I didn't want to know about. Although I was upset when that mammogram found a small cancer, I wasn't surprised. My children did cry at my bedside, but it was because they were so glad to see me home again after my surgery." She smiled, "Since then I have visualized tiny white knights running any cancer cells out of my body and my children help me with that. They think it is fun to help 'cure' Mommy. However, the cancer was caught so early that there's every reason to believe I'm completely cured. I thank the psychic scan made it possible for me to find it early."

Be an Aura Energy Field Reader

If you have ever felt that someone was staring at you, if you have felt that eyes are boring into the back of your head, or taken an instant dislike/like to someone within a few seconds of meeting them, you may have been sensing that person's energy field. If you feel nervous during electrical storms, feel the energy in an empty room, or feel drained by the presence of someone you don't even know, you may be a psychic aura reader.

Auras are thought to be the visible manifestations of the vibrations, or energy fields, that surround every object in the world, living and nonliving. If you can see a person's aura, which changes as rapidly as emotions and thoughts change, and reflects the individual's physical, emotional, mental and spiritual condition, you can understand that individual more completely. An aura cannot be manipulated or faked. It shows true feelings and intentions.

You may have once seen an aura around someone, or felt an energy which gave you clues to the person, but you haven't managed to manifest that experience again. If so, you may want to practice some of these exercises:

Mind's Eye Aura Viewing

Experiencing an aura intuitively is viewing it with your mind's eye.

- Close your eyes, relax. Don't forget to relax your tongue. Take a few deep diaphragmatic breaths.
- Visualize the person whose aura you want to see.
- Does a color come immediately to mind in association with that individual? If you think:

> She is always so sunny
> He's always so dark and gloomy
> She's a firecracker
> He was green with envy
> She is feeling blue,

you will immediately understand that you may be intuitively sensing the person's aura and are describing that, as well as their usual emotional state.

- As you think of a person, surround them in the color you usually associate with them and then focus on more detail.

You may begin to see drifts of other colors in the background as you concentrate. When you first see an aura, the predominant effect is of the person's physical health, and the more symmetrical the radiations, the physically healthier the person. A lack of symmetry indicates an imbalance and will reflect the individual's energy in the physical world. Other radiations will indicate moods, emotional states and the person's spiritual health, and are usually seen as flares of color running through the ruling field.

You will find that these intuitive auras are usually quite accurate.

It is thought that many religious paintings and illustrations that show a halo around the head of individuals are proof that there was a time when the visibility of auras was taken for granted. The auras of those individuals whose goodness actually emanated in a beautiful golden glow could be clearly seen by most people.

In the practice of viewing auras or energy fields, it is believed that the physical field is easier to both see and feel. With additional practice, you will be able to view or feel the other six fields as well: the two mental, two emotional, the astral, and the two etheric or vital fields.

With practice, reading auras can become as easy as reading body language, giving you an additional tool to understand other people's thoughts and emotions.

Feeling Your Own Energy Field

Since auras are said to be the visible manifestation of energy fields, try to feel your own energy field before you attempt to see it. This will prepare you for feeling or viewing the energy fields or auras of others.

- Sit relaxed in a comfortable chair, take a few deep breaths, center yourself, and briskly rub your hands together.
- Now cup your hands together, finger tips almost touching, heels of the palms almost touching. Feel the warmth you

have generated. Close your eyes and concentrate on the feeling in your hands and fingers.

- Slowly separate your hands and feel the energy between them as you move them farther apart and then closer together, almost touching. You might feel as if your hands are magnetized—that when you move them within a couple of inches of each other they seem to be resisting.

Try this exercise several times during the day to become aware of your own energy shifts as your energy field expands and contracts, along with your own emotional states. As you practice, you will become aware of subtle changes in your own energy field that will correspond to how you are feeling at that moment.

You will find that sometimes you can feel the energy as far away as six inches. At other times, your fingertips will be almost touching before you feel your own energy.

These energy fields have been described as ever-changing. At different times they may feel dense, flowing, blocked, tingling, vibrating, bubbly, or like an electric shock. You may feel as if your palms are filled with iron filings, operating like tiny magnets, attracting and then repelling each other.

After you have experienced your own energy field, felt it expand and contract, you may be ready to see your own aura or energy field.

Viewing Your Own Energy Field

Auras are seen with peripheral or side vision rather than the central part of vision. You will be using the cells in your eyes known as rods rather than with the cells called cones. The rods in the eye are sensitive to low levels of light rather than the bright light of daytime where the use of the cone cells predominates. Because we have been taught to focus intently on the things we want to see—computer screens, books, the roadway before us—it may take a while to release the dominance of your central vision and let your peripheral vision take over.

Looking straight ahead, extend your arm out in front of your face with the index finger pointing up. Slowly move your arm to the right while you still look straight ahead and note where your field of vision ends. This is where your peripheral vision begins. This is where auras are seen.

To begin energy field viewing:

- Sit relaxed in a comfortable chair, take a few deep breaths, center yourself and lean over, resting your arms on your knees with your hands hanging freely from the wrists. Slowly bring your fingertips together in front of you, touching your index fingers to each other lightly.
- Gaze, without blinking, at a place on the floor just beyond where you can see your fingers connected. Using the kind of unblinking stare we often associate with daydreaming, soften your focus, (which will blur your vision slightly) and slowly separate your fingertips no more than one inch apart.
- Gaze, unblinking, at the area on the floor between your fingertips. Now move them slowly, a little apart, a little closer together, then apart again.

It may take several minutes, but you will see wisps of energy, like smoky trails, connecting your fingertips to each other. Don't expect this visible aura to stay in sight. It may flash or pulsate, and then vanish before you are even sure you have seen it.

You have now seen a small portion of your own aura, which actually surrounds your body completely. With some practice, you will begin to see that this mist or smoky trail has color. As you become aware of color, you will find that your energy field changes color as you move from one level of consciousness to another, from one level of awareness to another.

When you are comfortable seeing your aura as it extends from your fingertips, you can practice the same with your hands and your forearms, bringing them together and then separating them, until you see this mist between them, giving yourself a larger portion of your own aura to view.

Be patient and continue practice—you are just beginning your aura viewing experience.

Full Aura Viewing

Once you have learned to observe the energy field traveling between parts of your body—fingertips, knees, forearms—you will want to view your own aura fully.

- Stand in front of a mirror in very soft light, similar to twilight. It helps if the background is one solid color, not a busy or distracting pattern such as flowered wallpaper. Take a deep breath, center yourself and soften your focus. Look, not at your reflection in the mirror, but over your left shoulder to a spot on the wall behind you. Your reflection should be just on the edge of your peripheral vision. Don't blink— gaze with a daydreamy kind of softened focus. You should not force this exercise. At first you may feel a little self-conscious, as many of us do, staring at ourselves in the mirror because our egos become involved. Try for a few minutes and then let it go. As you become more comfortable with the process you will find it easier. Soon you will see your own aura.
- Try changing your mood by adding music, holding a crystal or perfuming the air. You may be surprised to find how much even subtle changes in your environment can affect recognizable changes in your aura, its color, its flares, its area of extension beyond your physical self.

The Aura of Others

Viewing other people's auras is done in the same manner. In order to view auras you need to be relaxed, centered and comfortable.

Try this in a restaurant.

- Look at a stranger in a group who is busy talking to companions, someone who will be unaware of you, so you won't be caught staring. People sitting against a window, where the light is coming in on them, are the best subjects.
- Take a deep breath, center yourself, blur or soften the focus of your vision slightly and gaze just over the person's shoulder. With your eyes slightly unfocused, you may be able to see their aura around their head, or along the side of their head and shoulder.

Beginning aura viewers usually see wisps of smokelike material that is almost colorless. This is normal because you have not fine-tuned your auric vision as yet—but it is a beginning. As you work, you will find that the colors will become increasingly clearer.

Companion Aura Viewing

Ask a friend to share an aura viewing exercise. Try to see each other's aura by gazing just over each other's shoulders against a dark background in some dim light. Your aura viewing will improve as you give each other feedback about what you see.

Once you have seen the aura emanating from your own fingertips or from another individual, you will no longer doubt the existence of these energy fields. You will have found a new way to experience what we call intuition of the sixth sense—a visible manifestation of your psychic self.

Be open to the energy fields of others, learn to experience the energy fields of the universe.

The colors of the auras have a diversity of meaning. Subtle shadings and intensities, depth, vibrancy and location can change those meanings. Where they are in relationship to each other, how strong or intense, whether they indicate an emotional state, a physical condition, or a thought process, every aura has a complex variety of information to show you. Only practice with aura reading will give you the meanings of those differences. Here's a starting point for understanding what is generally said to be revealed by the colors of an aura:

Color	Meanings
Red:	Strength, passion, love, anger, hate, aggression, impulsiveness.
Pink:	Compassion, love, purity, comfort, modesty, immaturity, truthfulness.
Gold:	Devotion, harmony, enthusiasm, inspiration, spirituality.
Orange:	Creativity, agitation, pride, vanity, courage, joy, gregariousness.
Yellow:	Optimism, wisdom, intellect, enthusiasm, psychic, critical, dogmatism.
Green:	Sensitivity, compassion, reliability, dependability, strength, friendliness, healer.
Blue:	Calmness, loneliness, devotion, honesty, worrying, fearfulness, domineering.
Violet:	Intuition, practicality, humility, strength, overbearing, independence, spirituality.
White:	Truth, purity, awakening, creativity.

Gray:	Femininity, illumination, imbalances, secretive, loner.
Brown:	Growth, industry, organization, ill health.
Black:	Shielding, secretive, understanding, imbalances, substance abusers.
Glitter or sparkles:	Creativity, fertility.

Some New Age shops sell aura or chakra goggles; some people have found them to be useful. These glasses are made with colored lenses—orange, blue, purple, etc. The theory behind the glasses is that they have an effect on the sensitivity of the rods in the eye and will speed up your ability to see auras. If you have sunglasses with colored lenses, you might try viewing auras through them, to explore whether or not they help.

Lorraine and Sue—Tossing Energy

Sue, an engineer, and Lorraine, a tarotologist and writer, had been experimenting with various psychic experiences for several months. Lorraine now was sure she felt her energy between her hands and she had also seen her own aura in the mirror. Sue had felt the energy but had not yet seen her aura or anyone else's.

The women were eating dinner in a restaurant when they decided to test their energy fields. Lorraine rubbed her hands briskly together and then made a balling motion with her hands. "I'm compacting some of my own energy here," she said. "I want you to look at my hands and see my aura."

Sue looked but she could see nothing.

"Look, I am holding a small glowing ball," Lorraine said, cupping her hands together and showing them across the table to Sue. "Try to intuit what color it is."

Sue thought for a moment. "I'm sorry, I don't see a thing," she replied.

"Don't think!" Lorraine said, "Intuit! Feel it. What's the first thing that comes to your mind?"

"Green?" Sue said, hesitantly.

"Right!" Lorraine smiled. "Don't think too much. You want to use your intuition, your sixth sense. Now watch." Lorraine softly threw her little green invisible ball toward the back of the man seated at the next table.

In amazement, Sue watched as the man turned and smiled hesitantly in their direction, then nodded his head before turning back to his table companions. "What happened?" she asked.

"I sent him some of my energy—enthusiasm and friendliness," answered Lorraine, "and I guess he felt it. Now, you try it."

Sue felt a little foolish, but she rubbed her hands together, willing them to hold some of her energy, and then threw it across the room to a woman who was eating alone and appeared to be absorbed in reading a book. To Sue's surprise, the woman raised her head quickly and looked directly into her eyes. "I was embarrassed," she said. "I had to look away myself because I didn't know how to react."

Sue says they have performed their aura exercise dozens of times since then and it has worked every time. "Once I was feeling really irritable. When I threw my energy at a man, he got up and walked by our table, glowering at us. I was frightened for a minute, and then I realized that it is not a good idea to try this if you are going to send your negative energy to someone."

Lorraine nodded in agreement. "We recognize that we should treat this power with great respect. Now we only do it when we are capable of sending out friendship and healing to our fellow human beings."

Strengthen Your Psychic Energy

By relaxing, expanding and strengthening your own energy field you will be able to bring psychic energy to you. You will attain the ability to read auras and to experience psychic visions, dreams, and synchronicities.

Many psychic believe that it is important to vitalize and strengthen your own aura. They also believe that it is important to avoid people with negative energy, to expose yourself to sunlight and fresh air, practice healthy breathing, get some physical exercise, eat a healthy diet, meditate, fill your home with good fragrances, listen to soothing music, avoid drugs and alcohol, and carry a double-terminated crystal (one with points on both ends). It's always a good idea to improve your lifestyle, whether or not you want to access your sixth sense.

Recirculate Your Own Energy

We have all seen the photos of yogis, sitting with legs crossed and the tips their thumbs and index fingers touching. Centuries of practice have taught them that this posture is beneficial because it keeps their psychic energy circulating within their own bodies. If you feel drained of energy, this is a good position to take to keep your own psychic energy recirculating. Or you might place the palms of your hands together with your feet on the ground, connected with the earth's energy. Breathe deeply and center yourself and you will find your energy recharged, your balance and grounding maintained. This will aid in developing your psychic sensitivity.

Plant Energy Exercise

It does not matter if you believe you have a black thumb, or if you have been unable to keep plants alive before. You will be amazed at what you will learn from this exercise about your ability to care for and nurture a simple house plant, another living part of the universe.

Kirlian photographs, which purport to show the subtle energy field emanating from every living thing, are beyond the scope of the average photographer. But it is possible to see with your own eyes the ability of plants to respond to your emotions and subtle energy—to respond to your life force with an increase in their life force.

- Select two house plants as close to each other in size and conditions as you can. Pick out plants that have a reputation for being easy to grow and care for, ones that do well indoors. If you wish to be absolutely certain they are identical, you might repot them when you bring them home.
- Place these two plants in similar locations in your house so that they will receive equal amounts of sunlight and water, and then water and fertilize them the same way. Treat both plants with respect but do nothing extra for one—only water and feed it.
- For thirty days: Water and fertilize both plants identically.
- Select one plant, and for the entire time of the exercise, lavish it with praise. Pick it up, bring it close to your face as you admire it. Sing to this plant. It doesn't matter what you sing, it could be your favorite song at the moment, or one that has nice memories attached to it or something from your childhood. Say to your chosen plant, "How beautiful you are, you are my favorite plant. I can't imagine anything more beautiful than watching your leaves uncurl, seeing your blossoms just waiting to open. I look forward every day to seeing how big and strong and beautiful you are growing." There is nothing magic in these particular words, because of course the plant doesn't understand language, they are just suggestions of what you might say. You can say anything you wish, tell the plant about your day, about a book you have just read, about what you are going to watch later on TV but convey the *emotion* of feeling and caring. This will alter your energy field in a positive way so

that you will send out an energy field that encourages the plant to be healthy and strong.

- Put a small mark on the table, so that when you put the plant back down, you are placing it in the exact same spot every time.

- As you talk and sing to your plant, feel your energy going toward it, loving it, valuing it, caring for its growth, health and well being as if it were your child. Have regard and appreciation in your heart for its development. Give the plant five minutes of your time, every day.

- At the end of thirty days examine both plants objectively. Ask someone who doesn't know about your experiment to take a look at the two plants and tell you what they see. You will both be amazed at the differences. The plant you have energized will be noticeably healthier, larger and more beautiful.

Think what it could mean to be use your energy field in positive ways, to able to contact and affect the energy fields of others around you! Perhaps you can practice using this to affect and alter the mood of a miserable boss, an unhappy husband, a cranky baby, a sulky teenager. Or you could use your energy to telepathically request a raise, get a car loan approved, get the woman you have been admiring from afar to say yes when you ask her out.

Once you become aware of your own energy changes, once you have seen your own aura and that of other living creatures, you cannot doubt that auras and energy fields exist. Now you can choose to consciously increase your vitality, expand your energy field, increase your opportunities to connect with the psychic power of the collective unconscious that is always out there, waiting to break through to you.

Although we all have psychic powers, some of us are more talented in one area than another. You may have already communicated with someone telepathically, or gotten a strong feeling when someone handed you something personal of theirs, such as their car keys or a family photograph.

The following are two experiments you can try, to see if one of these areas is more developed in you than others. For many, finding that they have a particular route to the paranormal is the way to enter into the experience more readily. And from there, additional skills can be developed.

Telepathy Exercise

Telepathy works in both directions. Not only can you receive messages from someone, they can receive them from you. If you feel you have a particular affinity for this area of psychic power, you might want to try sending a telepathic message to a friend who is also interested in telepathy.

- Agree upon a time when one of you will be the receiver and the other the sender.
- The sender should select an object, such as a favorite piece of clothing, jewelry or a photograph.
- Both of you should sit quietly and relaxed for about ten minutes.
- The sender should concentrate on the object and try to project its image to the receiver. Concentrate on all the details of the object, including everything you know about it from all of your five senses: how it looks, if it makes any sound, its color, weight, taste and texture.
- The receiver should allow any thoughts to enter his/her mind at random and let them pass through quietly.
- At the end of the experiment, the receiver should tell the sender the best overall impression received, such as the color of the object or whether it was soft or hard.

If any of the information is correct, you and your partner in the experiment can congratulate yourselves that you have been telepathic—and you can practice again for more detail. You will find that you will improve with practice.

Lost Love Telepathy

In this exercise, you will try to contact another person. It might be someone you haven't seen in a long time, but would like to. It could be someone you wish would call, but with whom you might feel uncomfortable initiating the contact.

- Select a time, perhaps just before bedtime. Each day at this regular time sit quietly, breathe deeply, center yourself, relax and picture this person in your mind. See them sitting down writing a letter to you or picking up the telephone to call you. Picture them as completely as you can. If you know what their home looks like, where the phone is located, visualize them in that place. Concentrate on sending them this message: "Hello, . . . I would like to hear from you." If you have a particular question you would like answered, send that in your message too. Feel your energy going out to them and visualize them lifting up their head and looking in your direction as they "hear" you.
- Conduct this little telepathy exercise for one week.
- If you hear from the person, you know now that telepathy is very powerful. If you do not hear from them, give them a call or write. Don't be surprised if the first thing they say is, "I was just thinking about you!"

Clairvoyance

Closely related to telepathy is clairvoyance, the ability to access information about events that are happening at that moment. Many people have their first psychic experience when there is a major disastrous event, such as an earthquake, a fire, or an airplane crash. This is because there is so much psychic energy being generated. That energy sends out a strong signal that breaks through to consciousness.

If you are interested in clairvoyant experiences, you can often begin accessing these moments with someone with whom you have a close connection. The clairvoyant connection between twins is well known—often they sense when something is happening to their twin at the moment it occurs. More often than not, twins appear to be joined by an invisible psychic link that can operate even when they are thousands of miles apart.

Twins Rick and Ron and Telepathy

Rick and Ron had done almost everything together for most of their lives, including dressing alike, playing the same sports and dating startlingly similar girls. They had never been separated for long periods of time. But after they graduated from college, both with degrees in computer science, Rick took a job with an international real estate company and moved to Spain to begin his professional life. Ron took a job with a computer software company in a town close to home in Ohio. The separation was painful for both, but they knew the time had come to live as individuals instead as a pair. They spoke frequently on the phone and looked forward to getting together for vacations.

Ron said, "I woke up in the middle of the night with an excruciating pain in my head that traveled down my neck. I sat up in bed and felt my arms and hands suddenly go numb. I remember calling out for help before I fell back on the bed and passed out. When I woke up in the morning my mother was standing beside my bed and I could tell by the look on her face that something was terribly wrong."

Ron put his hands over his face for a moment, "I didn't have to ask. I knew. I said, 'Something has happened to Rick.' Although I knew what she would tell me, my mother had a hard time getting the words out. My brother was dead. He had been attacked and hit over the head by a thief in the streets of Barcelona and died at the hospital of his injuries at the exact time I felt that terrible pain in the middle of the night."

Ron believes in the communication between twins and says, "I miss him a lot, of course, but I still feel like Rick is with me. Quite often I get the feeling that he is right at my side, guiding and directing me."

Clairvoyance Connection

You can practice connecting to anyone anywhere in the world, instantly.

- In a quiet place, think of the person you want to access. A child away at college, a parent who lives in another state, a friend who is traveling. Visualize the person, picture the whole person as clearly as you can. Think about them at that moment. See them engaged in what they would usually be doing at that time of day—eating breakfast, driving to work, walking the dog.
- Ask a question: "How do you feel?"
- Be prepared to feel an emotional response. Be open to the experience. Perhaps you will suddenly feel sad, or find the corners of your mouth are turning up in a smile.
- Ask the question a second time: "How do you feel?"
- Be prepared for the answer to surface within your own

physical self. You may feel actual physical symptoms. Do
you feel a headache coming on or an ache in your knees?

- If you can, call your subject and find out if your feelings
  are accurate. That is the only way you can know if you have
  accessed them psychically.

Sometimes, if there is an emergency, these feelings will be vivid
and startling. But in an exercise such as this it is seldom that you
will tune in to such an experience.

Clairvoyant images are often ephemeral; before you are aware
of them, they are gone again. So pay close attention, allow whatever
surfaces to emerge, and write your impressions down before they
can fade away. Every time you are right, record that in your psychic
journal so that you begin to get a feeling of how well you are doing
at being clairvoyant.

Perhaps you have connected with someone. If you have, it is a
wondrous thing that can start you on your psychic journey. This
clairvoyant journey can create a connection that is intimate and
beyond the known five senses, creating an bond that is stronger,
deeper and more loving and caring than you may have experienced
before.

Personal Object Psychometric Exercise

You can practice discovering information in your mind from
holding another's possession.

- Ask someone to give you a piece of their jewelry—a watch,
  a ring, a bracelet, something they have been wearing and
  to which they have a strong attachment. The object can
  also be car keys, a photo they carry in their wallet, anything
  that has been in contact with their energy field and has
  significance for them.

- Hold the jewelry or object in your hand. Close your eyes and ask the owner to close their eyes and relax too.
- Tell the owner that you are going to say whatever comes into your mind. It doesn't matter how strange what you might say seems to you. Ask them to say yes if anything you say has any meaning to them. As you hear their voice with only that one word, you may be aware of subtle differences in tone as what you report is accurate.
- Close your eyes, take a deep breath, center yourself and begin. Say whatever comes to mind, talk until you have no more images or impressions.

You may be surprised at what develops from this experiment. If you have connected with or been accurate in even one or two items, then you know that this is an avenue of the paranormal that will open for you.

You can use psychometry to find lost people or objects, to uncover forgotten memories, to reveal thoughts and even hidden emotions. This can be an excellent way to know how people really feel about emotional situations and help make difficult decisions.

Iris and Her Long Lost Brother

Iris, a young woman with beautiful curly hair, came to see Mae and brought a photograph of her brother.

"My brother Jim has been missing for twenty years. He walked out of the house one day when he was seventeen and we never heard from him again. My parents made a missing person's report and searched for years, but it was as if he had vanished off the face of the earth. My mother isn't very well now, and I'd like to find him even though it may turn out he's dead," she said wistfully.

Mae took the picture in her hand and looked at the image of the tall, lanky boy, leaning against a tree in the yard, his arms folded across his chest, a defiant look on his face. The photo was well worn because Iris had carried it with her for years, showing it to people in the hope that someone might recognize her brother.

"Of course, I know he doesn't look like this anymore, but it is the last picture taken of him before he vanished," she said. "Is he dead, do you think?"

Mae closed her eyes and held the photo against her heart. She said, "No, I believe he is alive. I see ships, cargo ships. Did you live someplace near a marine or a dock?"

"Yes," Iris answered, "We lived near the port in Ft. Lauderdale, Florida at that time, near the place where the cruise ships left regularly to go all over the world."

Mae said, "I have an image of an onion, a large one."

They looked at each other. "What could that mean?" asked Iris.

"I don't know," answered Mae. "Sometimes the symbols are understood only after you think about them. You need to free associate, work on it for a while."

Iris left disappointed, although she was pleased to think that her brother might still be alive. Mae was confident that she had given her valuable information. Iris just didn't understand it yet.

Some months passed until Iris arrived once again at our door. When Mae opened it, Iris threw her arms around her and began hugging and kissing her. "You are absolutely amazing, I can't believe it," she cried.

When Iris calmed down enough to talk, she told Mae that she had gone home and puzzled over the image of the onion for several days, but it didn't mean anything to her. "I tried free association but that didn't do anything. I tried to think if my brother liked or hated onions, or if there was ever anything that had happened that involved onions, but nothing came to me. I thought it over and finally decided it was just meaningless nonsense. But still, it kept surfacing in my thinking. When I went to the grocery store, of course, I looked at onions. I saw white ones, green ones and shallots and chives. But it wasn't until I talked to the produce manager that it suddenly struck me. What you saw was a Bermuda onion!

Bermuda—a *place!* I was so excited. It seemed like a silly thing to do, but I took my vacation there to see if I might accidentally find my brother. I had never been there before so I decided I'd enjoy myself even if nothing turned up. It was pointless to search the entire world for my brother but Bermuda isn't very big. Since we have a rather unusual last name, it didn't take very long to find Jim." Iris paused to wipe the tears from her eyes. "It's a long story, but he has a small business there—and a wife and three children!"

"So what happened twenty years ago?" Mae asked.

"Well, he had a fight with my father over something silly, just like a lot of kids, so he decided to run away from home. He went down to the dock, and because he was big for his age, had a driver's license and some other identification, no one questioned him too closely. He got a job on a cargo ship and ended up in Bermuda. He says he thought often of contacting my parents, but as the years went by it got harder and harder for him to think of doing that, apologizing and all. He was thrilled that I had found him! He talked on the phone for several hours with our parents. Now my parents are going to Bermuda to meet their daughter-in-law and the grandchildren they never dreamed they had. It is going to be a wonderful reunion!"

Psychokenesis

A basic law of physics says that to move any object there must be an expenditure of energy. Normally, you move an object by picking it up and shifting it to another place. But what if you could move something or someone without physical touching, but by using the energy fields that are all around us? How can you tap into this energy and direct it toward an object? Those who are familiar with the martial arts such as karate, kung fu and tai chi have seen demonstrations of the ability of those known as masters or *sensei* to break boards or bricks with their bare hands. The *sensei* practices great mental discipline, internally focuses all his energy in the solar plexus and then outward. The *sensei* pushes forward mentally from that point, increasing the energy, increasing the concentration, focusing energy outward from the point where the third chakra is said to be located, bringing all the physical energy at his command to the object, to accomplish something which would, on the surface, appear to be impossible.

Athletes work with professional psychologists to focus and visualize about their sports, seeing themselves winning as they are directing the action of their muscles. Focusing on directing the ball in tennis, golf and baseball are examples where gaining psychokinetic control over an object can be useful.

Another way to put psychokenesis to work accessing the forces of the universe is to use a Ouija board. This board has the alphabet and other symbols on it, and a planchette (a pointer), that is thought, when touched with the fingers, to move in such a way that it spells out messages in response to questions. Because the Ouija board was originally marketed as a game, it is thought by many to be no more than that. Therefore, individuals who do not take it seriously can play tricks on other participants by moving the pointer to the answers they desire rather than allowing messages to come through spontaneously. If you wish to seriously use the Ouija board as a means of accessing the psychic realm, it is best to work individually or to participate only with people who are serious about using the board as a psychic tool.

Another good example of psychokenesis is Qigong, the amazing healing from China, in which the powerful energy system of the body which flows through known energy pathways is controlled and manipulated. Qigong masters are said to be able to control their energy so well that they can actually push another individual twice their size across the room by the effort of their *qi* (energy).

In *Miracle Healing from China: Qigong,* Dr. Charles McGee asked a Qigong master, Dr. Effie Poy Yew Chow, what it felt like when *qi* was activated. Dr. Chow answered:

"It can be felt in the form of heat or a quick surge of energy. It might be a tingling sensation, heat or warmth moving slowly through the body with a sense of tranquillity. The palms generally feel warm, or even hot, with a tingling sensation which is often felt most strongly in the hands and fingertips. Energy emanations, the colors and intensity of electromagnetism, or a corona may be seen coming from the body."

Dr. McGee asked: "What are you doing when you temporarily cause people to lose muscle strength and are able to push even large men around?"

"It may look as if I am doing something to weaken people, but I am not," Dr. Chow replied. "I sense the strength and direction their force is moving and breathe with my diaphragm. I combine their force and my own force to direct a powerful action in the direction I want."

Compass or Marble Psychokenesis Exercise

Psychokenesis can be used to move small objects. Once you can accomplish this, you can move on to larger ones.

- Imagine that the object before you is not solid, but is made up of waves of energy. It is vibrating or oscillating rapidly although you cannot see it.
- Place a small compass on the table in front of you and wait until the needle has aligned itself with the magnetic field of the earth.
- Focus your attention to the very tip of the needle. Relax, center yourself, and then concentrate on finding the energy of the needle. Then, try to combine it with your own energy.
- Move the needle clockwise.
- Focus your thinking on the solar plexus area of your abdomen and feel your energy flowing outward, joining with the needle's energy. Some psychics have said that they mentally ask the object to help them and guide them in the movement.

- If the needle wavers at all, you have effectively moved it psychokenetically. Now try moving it in the other direction.
- Using a washable pen, put a small dot on a table. Place a round object, such as a marble, on the dot in front of you. The purpose of the dot is so that you can measure any movement of the round object.
- Gather your energy, enlist the energy inherent in the marble and move the marble, just as you did in the compass needle exercise.

Any movement at all, no matter how tiny, is a beginning and a success.

Coin Control Exercise

Practice influencing the outcome in the flipping of a coin. Once you can accomplish this you can move on to bigger and better things such bingo, lottery wheels or slot machines.

- Select a coin at random.
- Determine which side you want to land up: heads or tails.
- Relax, center yourself and as you flip the coin, connect with the energy of the coin, look at the direction in which it is spinning and connect with that direction. Then, direct your energy from your solar plexus toward the coin, willing it to land on the side you desire.

   (Your chances of being correct are fifty percent for heads, fifty percent for tails.)
- Write down how often you are correct. Anything over fifty percent landing on the side you selected can be considered an effective display of psychokenesis.

Controlling Games of Chance

Everyone wants to win at the casinos. You must remember that most of these casinos have programmed their equipment to favor the house, so the odds are already set against you.

However, you can try the same concept. For example, a roulette wheel is spinning in one direction, the ball is spinning in the other. Is it possible to connect their energies with yours at the proper moment in the apex all of these oscillations—and win? It certainly would be fun to try but remember, you should never bet more than you can afford. Should you suddenly start winning, you will find that the management will be very interested in you and your activities.

Ralph and Clearing the Highway

Ralph travels the interstate many hours a week in his job as a salesman for a food company. "I try to take it easy, stay within the speed limits, and still get my work done," he says. "I have watched the highways get more and more clogged with traffic and I've been stuck behind big eighteen-wheelers lots of times. When I complained, Mae suggested that I try to move the traffic around with my mind. I just laughed at the idea but then one day I was so frustrated with highway delays I decided that I ought to give it a try."

"What did you do?" I asked.

"At first I mentally asked the other driver to move over or to take the next exit and get out of my way, but nothing happened. So I decided to try mentally pushing them over to the side of the road." Ralph held up his big hands, "Nothing rough, you understand, I just focused my energy on the driver, not the vehicle, and eased them over. At first I was very surprised to see cars pull into the slower lanes and let me pass. I've been perfecting it for a couple of years now and I find if I do it without anger, it works better than if I let myself get annoyed with the other drivers. I've also learned to give them a mental, 'Thank you' as I pass.'' Ralph grinned. "Everyone who has to spend any time on the highway should try it. It works!"

Most of us are aware of Israeli Uri Geller's claims that he can bend spoons and start stopped watches with this kind of energy—demonstrations he performs to show that he can psychokenetically control and move solid objects. While there doesn't seem to be much value in spoon bending, there are those, like Ralph, who say they can direct a traffic light to turn green as they approach it, who can always locate a parking spot when they need one, who claim they can even direct the play of lotto numbers. These are amusing examples of the practice of psychkonesis. You might want to experiment with making an empty parking spot appear when you want one, changing the traffic light in your favor, or directing the roll of the lottery balls.

Automatic Writing

Automatic writing takes place when you place your hand on a sheet of paper and allow something else to take over. There has been debate whether or not this writing comes from spirits, the subconscious of the individual, or from the collective unconscious of the universe. A pen that feels comfortable in your hand and a blank notebook are all that are necessary to attempt automatic writing.

Some authorities believe that automatic writing is best done with your nondominant hand—that is, if you are right-handed use the left and vice versa.

As in channeling, automatic writing requires that you be in a very relaxed state.

- Prepare a place that is comfortable and dimly lit where you will not be interrupted.

- Play some soft music that you find inspirational.
- When you are ready, place your hand holding the pen lightly on the notebook and wait.
- When your hand begins to move over the page, close your eyes. Do not look at what is being written and don't worry about whether or not you are staying within the lines or on the page.
- Permit your hand to move without guiding it, just as if you were attempting to answer questions with an Ouija planchette.
- In your mind, ask a question. Perhaps you want to know what you should do about a current situation or a specific problem, or you want to know about something in the future.

When you read what is written, you may be surprised by what you find. Sometimes the message is quite clear. If the message is unclear or you want more information, ask another question and wait for your hand to move again for the answer.

Your Psychic Direction

You might look upon these exercises as no more than games and that is okay. Experiment. Play. See if there is a particular direction or area of psychic phenomena that seems suitable for you, or that interests you more than others. Enjoy trying to connect with the energy of the universe and if you find that you feel more connected, less alone than you felt before, that certainly may be all that you need to encourage exploration. You have been invited to experience another dimension.

It is up to you.

SIX

Drugs, Music and Other Trash: Why Not Just Drop Some Acid and Get There Quicker?

For there is a music wherever there is a harmony, order or proportion; and thus far we may maintain the music of the spheres.

—Sir Thomas Browne in *Religio Medici*

Throughout history, almost every culture has sought ways to alter consciousness by experimentation with plant substances that yield many of the psychoactive drugs of today. Some of the most popular substances are: alcohol, cannabis, opium, cocaine, peyote, psilocybin, morphine, nitrous oxide, chloroform, barbiturates, amphetamines, tranquilizers, caffeine and nicotine. So why not do as others have done, use something that will either alter brain waves without any effort or bring another dimension closer into reality with a little chemical assistance? One good reason, of course is that drugs are illegal. But there are other reasons as well.

LSD

Users of lysergic acid diethylamide, the psychedelic drug known as LSD, a potent hallucinogenic, report that it evokes dreamlike changes in mood and thought, and alters the user's perception of time and space. In the 1960s LSD use was widespread among people who sought to alter and intensify their physical senses, to achieve insights into the universe, nature and themselves, and to intensify their emotional connections with others. This would appear to be the very thing that would make that instant connection with the sixth sense a psychically oriented person is seeking. But thirty years later it is obvious that it did not provide these things and many of the famous proponents of its use found it necessary to go into treatment or are no longer with us.

As one young man recently described it, "Hey, it's good stuff. I just try and catch some visuals." But he apparently had no desire for anything more serious than to experience a psychedelic light show inside his brain.

Peyote

Anthropologists have examined the use of peyote by certain Native Americans. These individuals are on a lifelong and serious mystical and spiritual journey, one which is very complex. First they must disengage from secular life and make a complete confession of all of their faults of recent living, and that is just the beginning. If they are unable to submit to this sometimes searing self psychoanalytical experience, the magic of the mushroom is not going to work. Joseph Campbell in *The Power of Myth* writes, "For these mystics peyote is not simply a biological, mechanical or chemical effect, but one of spiritual transformation. If you undergo a spiritual transformation and have not had lengthy preparation, you will have the terrible experience of a bad trip. There is a difference between the mystical experience and the psychological crackup—the difference is years of long preparation."

Psychoparmacology

Psychopharmacology is the study of the relationship between drugs and brain function. Studies in this field report that mind-altering drugs appear to do one of two things: They either exhaust brain chemistry, (creating such things as a dopamine imbalance, the neurotransmitter necessary for proper functioning of the central nervous system and needed for normal dreaming and visualizing), or they connect to a receptor that then blocks brain chemistry from making the usual connections within the brain. These connections are essential for everyday functioning because a lack of neurotrans-mitters prevents impulses from traveling from one neuron to the next. Long-term users, depending on their drug of choice, may find that their brain chemistry is altered, sometimes permanently, resulting in adverse mental states such as persistent psychosis, pro-longed depression, memory loss and faulty judgment.

University of Cambridge physicist Brian D. Josephson, who won a Nobel prize for his discovery of superconducting circuits, announced in 1995 that he was renouncing conventional physics to study psychic and mystical phenomena. Dr. Josephson had devised an improved method for calculating the influence of gravity on Doppler shifts—changes in the frequency of sound or light waves. He proposed that electrons might tunnel through a barrier of insulating material in the middle of a superconducting circuit. His scientific predictions proved to be accurate and won him the Nobel prize but he found the resulting acclaim that accompanies being a Nobel winner more distressing than gratifying. After a brief use of tranquilizers, he regained a measure of peace through transcendental meditation and he now writes and lectures on topics such as consciousness, spirituality, and the possible links between quantum mechanics, psychic phenomena and music. Ultimately, Dr. Josephson apparently realized what many others have: that chemically altering brain chemistry to decrease stress is detrimental to life and well-being. His drug use brought him no closer to a psychic experience.

As we already know, in order to access *alpha* brain waves, the ones which are present during daydreaming, fantasizing and visualization, we need to be in a state of relaxed, detached awareness. While some chemicals may contribute to relaxation, they seldom aid awareness. Rather, they decrease the ability to function rationally and impair cognitive judgment. To experience *theta* brain waves, the ones that hold memories, sensations and emotions as well as creativity and inspiration, we need to be in a trance, in dreaming sleep, or in deep meditation. This is where we can have peak experiences, spiritual insight and access psychic intuition.

It does not appear, from any known research, that mind-altering drugs can jump-start, increase, aid or in any manner facilitate the psychic experience. In fact, the opposite appears to be true. Those who claim to need such assistance may be victims of their own abnormal thinking, induced by the chemicals.

Optimum Experience with Music

Mystics, Zen masters and shamans have known for centuries that the arrangement of sound in ways that please the ear can be used to improve the quality of life. Sounds can soothe, ease, heal, promote relaxation and enhance both physical and emotional well-being. One of the most popular functions of music is to focus the listener's attention on patterns that are appropriate for creating a desired mood. This organized auditory information reduces the disorder we experience when random information creates anxiety and boredom. Music, seriously attended to, can induce what is known as a flow or optimum experience—a state of concentration so focused that it amounts to absolute absorption.

Although this story is mythological, it illustrates the power that certain kinds of beautiful music can have over us.

In Greek legend, Apollo, the god of prophecy, music, medicine and poetry, delighted the other gods with his ability to play the lyre, a stringed instrument similar to the harp. His son Orpheus was such an excellent musician that he had no rival among mortals. When he played and sang, his music enchanted the trees and rocks and tamed wild beasts. Even the rivers altered their course to follow him. When his wife Eurydice died, Hades, the ruler of the underworld, was so moved by Orpheus's music that he gave Eurydice her life back and returned her to her adoring husband. On Orpheus's death his sweet sounding lyre went up into the northern sky and became the constellation Lyra, containing one of the brightest stars in the sky, the brilliant white star Vega.

The Mozart Effect

Researchers at University of California, Irvine have proven that cognitive skills, including reading, abstract spatial abilities and creativity, all improve with certain musical experiences. When they played classical music for college students ten minutes prior to an I.Q. test, overall scores improved as much as 30 percent. They selected Mozart for these studies because they believed that his musical structure facilitates cognitive processing and stimulates intellectual and creative development. The effect is not limited to Mozart. Music of any of the classical giants such as Bach, Beethoven, Haydn, Strauss, Clementi and Schumann has been documented to create a phenomenon that has come to be known as *the Mozart Effect*. Listening to this music alters brain waves in such a manner that any person's ability to perceive and understand is expanded.

Arousal

While Mozart's musical structure expands and calms, other music can terrify and excite. Pan, the god of shepherds and flocks, invented the panpipes or syrinx and was said to be able to create a state of panic and fear with this instrument.

Aficionados of heavy metal music say that "it is music to bang your head by." Some lawsuits have resulted from the alleged effects of this music. One of the most well-known was the suit brought against lyricist Ozzy Osbourne, CBS Records, and several other parties by the parents of a sixteen-year-old fan. It was claimed in a lawsuit that the teen was prompted to shoot himself to death by the lyrics and the subliminal messages allegedly buried in the recording of the song "Suicide Solution." The courts dismissed the suit for several reasons, including speech protected by the First Amendment. Three or four other suits by parents of teen suicides against other musicians have resulted in similar dismissals. It might have been better if the lawyers and the experts had examined the effects of loud repetitive noise on these listeners' brain waves over a period of time, rather than the supposed subliminal messages hidden in lyrics.

Listening to music can be a highly emotional experience. Lovers look into each other's eyes when "their song" is playing and are transported, forgetting there are others on the dance floor. Warriors march into battle, energized and proud, when the band plays. Music is obviously a form of communication but what it communicates is not always obvious. It can penetrate the core of our physical being. Listening, we can sob, experience intense pleasure, or be plunged into a depth of gloom. Imagine a movie without a sound track. In a monster film, the music prepares us for the ghoul or terrifying creature who will jump out from behind the door, frightening and thrilling us. Everyone seems to know the theme from the movie *Jaws* that precedes the shark attacks. The long gaze into the eyes of the beautiful stranger, accompanied by the sound of many violins, lets us know that these two will soon fall in love. Music can instantly transform our whole existence, bringing images of other worlds and other times. Singing and dancing can draw groups of people together, direct their emotions and prepare them to work together, such as fishermen hauling in unison on heavily laden drift nets. Another instance where people can be incited to act together is warfare. The Incas used flutes and drums. In some other cultures attacks upon enemies were initiated by blowing horns and trumpets. The sounds produced by musical instruments may help prepare people to attack by arousing aggressiveness and at the same time terrifying the enemy, or sounds can be used to frighten away evil spirits or encourage a warrior to be brave in the face of overwhelming adversity.

It is generally agreed that music causes increased arousal in those who listen to it with any degree of concentration. Arousal brings about a variety of physiological changes, many of which can be measured. The electroencephalogram shows changes in brain waves. The electrical resistance of the skin decreases; the pupil of the eye dilates; breathing may become rapid or irregular. Blood pressure and heart rates rise. Muscle tone increases, often accompanied by a physical restlessness, particularly in the legs. A rare disease, musicogenic epilepsy, has been documented by neurologist Macdonald Critchley. His findings convincingly confirm the fact that music can have a direct effect upon the brain. It would seem that certain music, for particularly sensitive individuals, actually causes all the neurons in the brain to fire in synchronization, triggering a seizure.

For the psychic, wishing to reach that relaxed dreamy state that precludes intuition, stirring music is detrimental. Instead, if you wish to meditate and contact the sounds of the universe, CDs of natural sound—birds, wind and rain—accompanied by gentle flutes or violins, are available at all music stores. Any gentle music played very softly, almost inaudibly in the background, with no distracting drums and other stimulating instruments, may ease the transition to that relaxed state that welcomes the sixth sense—that meditative state where time seems to have slowed.

Dowsing Rods and Pendulums

Dowsing rods and pendulums act as amplifiers. They don't amplify sounds of course, they amplify energy fields, which are the music of the universe.

Since ancient times both of these instruments have been used to connect with the energy of the earth. Farmers hire dowsers to locate water to irrigate their land or find a good source of drinking water. During wartime dowsing rods have been used to locate underground mines and tunnels. Some utility companies train their repairmen in their use, just to be on the safe side when they are trying to locate underground water systems, trace the course of a flood, or plot the course of an underground river. But they can be used to find more than water. They can find minerals, energy fields, archeological sites, lost objects, and people.

Traditionally dowsing rods have been made from a forked willow branch, but it is possible to make one out of any forked tree branch. Just trim it so that the forks are of equal length and smooth away the bark so your hands can feel any small movement of the branch.

Pendulums are amplifiers, too. The astronomer Galileo established that the arc of a simple pendulum that swings back and forth under the influence of gravity remains constant, provided that the fixed point from which it swings remains constant. In the nineteenth century, French physicist Jean Foucault suspended a pendulum on a long wire from the dome of the Pantheon in Paris and demonstrated the rotation of the earth.

Dowsing rods and pendulums work on the same principle: they interact with energy fields. Both can be used to increase your sensitivity to these invisible fields. They act as antennae, making the force of subtle energy fields visible by their movement. They can also be used to connect to psychic energy to find answer to questions.

Dowsing an Aura

With a dowsing rod you can locate and measure another's auric field.

- Hold the rod out in front of you very lightly at shoulder height. Walk toward your friend with the rod pointing directly at him or her. Walk slowly closer. When you contact the field, the rod should dip slightly. You will be able to see it dip and feel it in your hands, letting you know that you are at the outer edge of the field.
- Your subject should also be able to feel when the rod enters their field, that their personal space has been entered.
- Try it with your subject's eyes closed, while holding a crystal, eating chocolate, or with different kinds of music playing in the background. There will be subtle differences and this will help you identify auric changes.

The Pendulum—An Amplifier for Force Fields

The pendulum can be useful for the beginning psychic because it acts as a very sensitive amplifier. It can be used to diagnose illness, to prescribe medicine, or to search for hidden objects.

Any object that is free to swing while hanging from a fixed point is a pendulum. Many psychics use pendulums to answer simple yes or no questions or to work with the chakras.

When using a pendulum for psychic purposes, it does not swing from a fixed point but from the hand of a person. Remember, the muscles of your arms are controlled by many tiny nerves and while you may not be aware of it, we are all continuously making microscopic adjustments in the position of our bodies. Thus, movement on the part of the psychic can influence the motion of the pendulum but ultimately the motion of the pendulum is a function of the interaction of three force fields—the subject, the psychic, and the pendulum itself, making the energy visible.

Pendulum Exercise

Use a pendulum to get answers to questions.

- Using a string about six inches long and a small stone, a button, a ring or a key hanging from its end, you can make a pendulum. Support your arm by resting your elbow on a table. Let the pendulum swing freely from your fingers until it is motionless.
- Empty your mind of all preconceptions. The more you keep your desires out of the process, the more accurate will be your pendulum answers. You do not want your biases to influence the answers you ask.
- Relax; muscle tension will affect the pendulum.
- Ask the pendulum a question which can be answered yes or no, and one to which you already know the answer, such as "Am I—years old?" or "Are we in a house?" You can decide from those answers what kind of a swing will give you a no or a yes answer.

  Most psychics report that a back and forth swing is most often a no response and a circular motion is a yes one, but you need to experiment to find what is correct for you and your pendulum.
- Now ask the question you really wish to have answered. The more specific you are, the better the response. Take care and think the questions out carefully.
- You might ask, "Is _____ a good person?" and get a yes answer. A better question might be "Is _____ a good person for me?" That answer might be very different.

Pregnancy Pendulum Test

A pendulum can be used to predict the sex of the baby by representing the yin (feminine) or yang (masculine) nature of the total energy field of the unborn child.

- Ask a cooperative pregnant friend to lie down.
- Hold the pendulum over her abdomen as close to the body without touching. Psychics report that a circular pendulum swing means the child will be female and a back and forth motion a male.

This is a fun test to perform with someone who already knows the child's sex through tests but hasn't disclosed it to friends. You won't have to wait months to find our whether or not you have been accurate.

Chakra Health Pendulum

Make the power of chakras visible with the use of a pendulum.

Holding a pendulum over the various chakras is a simple way to visualize the energy flowing in and out of them. Because the pendulum acts as a visible gauge of energy fields, holding it over the various charkas can be used as a diagnostic tool. With practice you will be able to observe subtle qualities in their energy. The rate of swing can give information about whether or not the chaka is open, blocked or totally closed. A rapid swing or osculation can indicate sadness, tension or ill health; a slower motion, peacefulness, happiness and good health. There are many subtleties to these motions and only practice will bring the experience necessary for interpretation.

Your Environment

Because music appears to unleash not only creativity but focused thinking and ultimately access to creativity, it is useful to create an environment that will be conducive to accessing your psychic powers, particularly if you are just beginning. If you are tired and cranky, irritated with the world, work or family, you are in a state that will not be favorable. Relax, create a space, a sanctuary for yourself. It is helpful to have a peaceful, meditative environment, one that will invite psychic experiences in. Create a nest, it doesn't have to be large, just a corner of a room will do, someplace where you can be uninterrupted, surrounded with colors you enjoy, pictures that please you, pleasant scents. Furnish that sanctuary with scrolls, paintings, statues, porcelains, silks, flowers, candles; any one of hundreds of beautiful things that give you joy and provide resonance to your life, because these things help to ground you. A family photograph, a small keepsake, a drawing from a child, a talisman or a treasure from your own childhood may be all that you require for this sanctuary to be symbolic of the solitude and comfort it provides. Play some soft and gentle music. Burn a sweet-smelling candle or some incense. Build an environment that is free from distractions and aimed at creating a mood that will evoke a sense of calmness, a place that will help eliminate the static of the outside world and assist you to be more acutely attuned to the energy of the universe. As you calm yourself, you will shift out of your workaday world, that pattern of viewing the world around you as frenetic and wild. Shift into calmness and serenity, a more naturally quiet and still state.

Mystical Places

Some psychics are more comfortable with a natural setting, surrounded by nature and the trees, bird sounds, the flowers and plants that grow there.

Perhaps you would like to travel to some of the mystical places in the world that have been reported to have mysterious powers that could energize and inspire you.

Although it is not known what the builders of Stonehenge, a prehistoric monument north of Salisbury, England, intended, people travel hundreds of miles to join others there for rituals that are performed regularly by present-day people who consider themselves druids. According to Celtic mythology, the power of Mother Earth is represented here. These four concentric groups of stones are the embodiment of a form that not only has mystical properties, but is a way to both focus and contain energy. The present-day druids speak of being grounded and centered in this lonely place on a raw and windswept plain. They feel that here they have connected with the ancient energy of the earth and those who performed rituals here hundreds of years ago. Here they can bring focusing energy to the solar plexus chakra. These present-day druids often do no more than ask questions of the universe and then wait inside the circles of stones for the answers to come.

There are many places on the earth where great energy is thought to be focused. The Black Hills of South Dakota in the western United States is considered of great spiritual importance by the Native Americans, perhaps because of the richness of its gold deposits and other minerals, and because it was considered sacred by their ancestors. Machu Picchu, a pre-Columbian Inca stronghold in the Andes in Peru—a series of terraces built around a central plaza and linked together by numerous stairways—is also said to have been a center used in ancient religious practices. The Taj Mahal, a beautiful mosque, meeting hall and mausoleum outside Agra in India, is thought to hold magical powers for lovers because it was built by a Mughal emperor to demonstrate his great love for his beloved wife Mumtaz.

But it isn't necessary to travel hundreds of miles to find a special mystical place. You can access psychic energy anywhere in the universe.

Whether it is the sanctuary of your own home, or an outside

place, under the moon and the stars or in bright sunshine, it could be any spot that you find charming and therapeutic and which will help you to focus: a beach, a small stand of trees, a hilltop from which you can view the sky. Any of these locales could be a psychic space for you, a place where you can sit quietly and comfortably, meditating and connecting, while you allow the energy to flow.

While it is wonderful to have such a place, a sanctuary, where you can center yourself when you are just beginning to get the feeling of your psychic powers, one that you can return to frequently to rest and refresh, it is not essential to the pursuit of contacting the universal consciousness. With practice, you can learn to access your sixth sense anywhere, at any time.

Understanding Emotional Psychic Images

Because psychic images and the information they bring occur within the mind, when you are in a highly receptive state, relaxed and focused, it is important that you do not misunderstand them.

The emotional content of psychic experiences can be extremely draining and exhausting, particularly if they relate to accidents or disasters. It is important that the psychic be emotionally healthy, well-grounded and ethically strong. If you are such a person, you can open yourself to this new world of positive experiences and creativity, insight and exhilarating perceptions with pleasure and understanding. It is important to think carefully about your psychic experiences to be sure you are not misunderstanding the meanings of your visions or dreams

Most psychics say that the test of this is the *content* of intuitive or psychic impressions. They are frequently impersonal but highly emotional and the impressions they bring are often quite clear and not couched in symbolism. When you are in this highly receptive state colors appear more vibrant and objects are often more clearly defined. Little details stand out with a clarity they don't seem to have in everyday life.

If your dreams or visualizations direct you to act out antisocial behaviors or if the words you hear in your head are dangerous to yourself or others, every serious and professional psychic will tell you that these are *not* psychic experiences. They are messages which are coming from your own subconscious, and they should never be followed.

SEVEN

Solving Crimes: Do Cops Really Want Your Help?

The more featureless and commonplace a crime is, the more difficult it is to bring it home.
—Sir Arthur Conan Doyle, in *The Adventures of Sherlock Holmes*

What an exciting thought—seeing yourself on television, being interviewed after you have solved a notorious crime or helped a family find a lost child. Accepting an award from a grateful police department and the governor of your state, or perhaps even from the president—because your psychic skills have made you famous!

Psychics often appear on television or in magazine articles, claiming to have helped the police solve the most unsolvable crimes. But Sue Kovach, in her recent book *Hidden Files—Law Enforcement's True Case Stories of the Unexplained and Paranormal,* writes that she found law enforcement authorities divided on the subject: while many said they would give consideration to psychic tips, far more said the information is vague at best and could never be used in court.

While the popular media often suggest that police departments in the United States welcome and use psychics for assistance in solving crimes, a recent survey of the police departments of the country's fifty largest cities revealed that 65 percent of these cities do not use and have never used psychics in criminal investigations. Moreover, no respondent said that psychics provided more useful information than was received from other sources. The comments of some respondents suggest that psychics may even hinder their investigations.

Roughly 35 percent of urban U.S. police departments and 19 percent of rural departments admit to having used a psychic at least once during their investigations. Other countries however, appear to be more willing to contact psychics for police investigations. Such psychic detectives are widely used in Britain, Holland, Germany and France. The authorities in these countries appear most willing to rely on information provided by psychics and find their assistance to be worthwhile.

The Boston Strangler

In the Boston Strangler case of 1964, then Attorney General Edward W. Brooke appointed a special investigative team to work with the Boston police after an eleventh victim was discovered. Brooke, under fire to catch this killer, called in Dutch psychic Peter Hurkos, "the man with the radar eyes and X-ray brain." Living in Hollywood, Hurkos had become known as the psychic to the stars, claiming his clients included such celebrities as Marlon Brando and Glenn Ford. Hurkos gave the police information that led to the arrest of Thomas O'Brien, who voluntarily committed himself to a mental hospital, making any prosecution impossible. Eventually Albert DeSalvo was arrested for a series of rapes, diagnosed as schizophrenic and committed to the same mental institution, where he eventually confessed to the Boston Strangler murders. Because he was declared insane, DeSalvo could not be prosecuted and the case was closed without a conviction. Hurkos always maintained that his identification of O'Brien had uncovered the real murderer, and he has never admitted to failure in this case.

Dorothy Allison—Locator of Missing Persons

Dorothy Allison is another well-known psychic who has worked with the police on a variety of cases, including some in which she has been surprisingly accurate. In the case of Deborah Sue Kline, who had been missing for months, Dorothy told police that they would find that fire would be very important to one of Debbie's two abductors. She said two men were involved, both had criminal records and were already in jail on other charges. She stated that the two men involved were named either Ronald or Robert or Richard; both are rapists and have double letters in their names. She told police that Debbie's body would be found on a hill and would not be completely buried. She also told them she saw the color yellow, a garbage dump, a shoe, and a plastic swimming pool. At the time none of this had any meaning to the investigators. However, when they later arrested Richard Lee Dodson, a man with a long criminal record, including rape, after being led to him by an informant, the police learned that Dodson had escaped unharmed from a fire that had burned his home to the ground, killing his wife and three children. He confessed to Debbie's murder and implicated Ronald Henninger as his accomplice. (Ronald and Richard had double letters in their names—Lee and Henninger.) Henninger's prior crimes also included rape and manslaughter. Dodson led police to the body, half buried in the snow on a hill, close to a dump site, past bright yellow highway warning signs. State troopers found a protruding shoe and Debbie's body partially covered by a blue plastic swimming pool.

In retrospect, Dorothy Allison was eerily accurate, but none of this information was helpful to the solution of the crime because it had no meaning until after the arrests.

"When you've reached a dead end, a psychic can help reinvigorate an investigation," says Captain Peter Person of the New York State Police, who first used Allison in 1992 to help find a fifteen-year-old girl who'd been missing for five years. "I was amazed," he adds, admitting that he was skeptical at first. "She got too many details right for it to be coincidental."

The walls of her home are covered with framed testimonials from police officers. And, although Dorothy herself says she has worked on 4,000 cases, she claims credit in only seventy-six of them.

Annette Martin—Totally Focused Psychic

Annette Martin, who set up an office doing psychic counseling and consulting to Gerald Jampolsky, a psychiatrist working on visualization techniques with cancer patients, has worked with the police numerous times. She describes how she does her psychic detective work. She says, "It is very easy to go into an altered state, it takes no time at all. I just take three deep breaths, my blood pressure drops, and I am totally focused on what I am doing. If you asked me to spell something—forget it. I cannot spell or write a word, but I can draw and I can verbalize. It used to be emotionally wearing but now it's exhilarating." The psychic believes that in the next ten or twenty years her methods are going to be commonplace as we make big strides in understanding how the mind works. Martin first experienced her psychic powers at age seven when some other children started throwing rocks at her. She heard a voice in her head and it told her, "Pick up that stick!" She knew her life would be changed if she obeyed the voice and so she picked up the stick, threw it, and those children ran way. That was the beginning for her—a voice telling her what action to take to protect herself, telling her what to do.

Nancy Myer-Czetli—Crystal Balls and Dead Bats

Nancy Myer-Czetli, a psychic who has worked on many police cases, describes in her book, *Silent Witness: The Story of a Psychic*

Detective, the sort of harassment experienced by the police officers who first used her assistance.

"Many were constantly serenaded with the theme to *The Twilight Zone,* and some of the officers found crystal balls and dead bats on their desks. When the media got wind of the fact that a psychic has been called in, the police are subject to ridicule whether or not they get results."

Nancy, who claims a success rate of 80 to 90 percent, says, *"Sometimes psychics are dead wrong."*

Many of the psychics who have worked with the police admit that while they are psychic, they are also human and can make mistakes. They must stay focused on functioning from the intuitive part of their minds only. If they begin thinking logically, analyzing the information or symbols they are receiving, their accuracy can vanish. Certain cases, such as those of missing children, can affect the psychic emotionally. The desire to solve these cases can sometimes distort perceptions.

Nancy also says, *"Time may be inexact."*

Just because the psychic gets an impression or fragments of an event does not mean that she knows if it has already happened or if it is a prediction for the future.

One of the most difficult parts for a psychic helping the police may be interpretation.

Nancy says, *"Interpretation of the impression may be very difficult."*

Even the most experienced psychic may receive accurate impressions but be unable to relate them to anything. Possibly no one else involved in the case can either, whether it is the victim's family, investigators, crime reporters, even the detectives most intimately involved in solving the crime. It could be information only the criminal knows, or something that the victim is experiencing. Often the impressions are just *there* and the psychic cannot tell where they are coming from.

Myer-Czetli says police crime photographs are extremely important to her. "When the police photographers are working, they circle the body, moving around and getting all the angles, and at some point they will stand, quite accidentally, in exactly the same spot in which the killer stood. It is that photo that gives me the most information, because I am able to see the victim as the killer saw him in those final seconds of life."

Some psychics go into the mind of the killer at this point, while others avoid doing that, but either way, by observing all the details in the photos, a psychic can sense things about the criminal, the way he thinks and operates, that can provide additional clues.

Official Positions on the Paranormal

For Marcello Truzzi, director of the Center for Scientific Anomalies Research and co-author with Arthur Lyons of *The Blue Senses, Psychic Detectives and Crime,* the attitude of officers' superiors may make working with psychics very difficult. Truzzi says, "Many officials in law enforcement have a great deal of nervousness about the 'giggle factor.' "

Many police departments have tried to keep their use of psychics secret, even when the psychic has been successful. They are surely going to deny using one if the psychic has failed. In addition, they may want to keep the credit for solving the crime entirely for themselves.

When Attorney General Janet Reno announced a two-million-dollar reward for information leading to an arrest in the case of the bombing of the Oklahoma City Federal Building, the toll-free number established at that time received thousands of calls. In other recent well-known cases which have received national attention, such as the brutal murder of O.J. Simpson's ex-wife Nicole, and when Ennis, the son of entertainer Bill Cosby was gunned down while changing a flat tire on the side of the road, law enforcement agencies set up toll-free tip lines. The chief of police in one such major case which had established a toll-free tip line said, "Unfortunately, national attention to a crime means that we get tips from

concerned citizens, from people who actually have information—
and also from every kind of paranoid nut and psycho out there.
We hear from people who have the straight scoop direct from Elvis,
and from people who might just be making some good guesses
but have absolutely no connection with the case and are calling in
with their idea of how to solve the crime based on what they have
read or seen on the nightly news. Many of these are well-intentioned
and sincere citizens who want to help the police and are anxious
to get a criminal off the streets. Of course we must follow up on
each and every one of these tips or leads, no matter how strange
they might seem at the time, because you never know where the
right lead is going to come from. What the general public doesn't
seem to understand is that this can not only cost thousands in
dollars and man-hours, it can even delay or actually hinder the
resolution of a case."

A recent case in point is the Oklahoma City case of Terri Schlatter
and her son Nathan, who had been missing for years. Following
information from an individual who claimed to be psychic, authorities
were led to a pond in a rural area of the state. The authorities
drained the pond, spent weeks digging, and ultimately abandoned
the search when no bodies were discovered. This kind of negative
result can discourage a police department's subsequent use of psychics.

Nancy Myer-Czetli, who has provided police with clues in a
number of crimes, says that after an experience with a Ouija board
in 1974 she found she could interpret the private thoughts of
everyone she encountered. She frequently uses the techniques of
telepathy and psychometry, reading the impressions stored in inanimate
objects. Two examples of her successes are the identification
of the murderer of a woman who was stabbed to death and the
discovery of the body of a man who had disappeared.

Sue Kovach tells us that while police solve crimes through conventional
methods they sometimes discover, after the fact, that a
psychic was accurate. There have been occasions when tips from

psychics caused the police to consider other directions for investigations.

"The police are more likely to accept information or guidance from a psychic when they have exhausted every possibility, when the case stays unresolved for years, or when they face increased pressure to solve a particularly notorious crime," said a police lieutenant in Lantana, Florida. "All they have to do is figure out which guidance will be useless and which will be helpful." He laughed. "And that's not so easy to do."

Mae and the Police

It was my mother's opinion that a good psychic can access information that the police might have overlooked or not understood. She believed that a psychic could telepathically access a kidnapper or a killer or the thoughts of the victim, but she feared that the emotional drain of being involved with crime might not be worth the emotional cost.

"By interviewing the detectives when they explain the case, the psychic can sense the significance of information. By viewing the crime scene and photos, or holding some of the victim's possessions, she can often provide valuable information. It might be information the police actually already have, details of the crime which at the moment are meaningless to them. They just don't know what they have," she said.

An example was a murder which took place in Michigan, in the late 1980s. A young woman was missing and her family was sure she had been murdered, but her body had not been found. The psychic, Cynthia, went with the detectives to the last place the woman had been seen. As they drove down a deserted road near her house, Cynthia told the detectives to stop. About 600 yards from that point, the body was found in dense shrubbery. Later, confronted with the discovery of the body, the victim's boyfriend confessed to her murder.

Law enforcement authorities were amazed. Cynthia said later that she had sensed a very subtle change in the body language of the detective driving the car. It was very subtle, but she was aware of it because, as any good psychic knows, you must pay attention to small details. It was the change in the detective's demeanor that caused her to ask him to stop where she did. When the detectives reviewed the facts in the case, they realized that they ought to have known, what Cynthia had intuited. These clues actually came from things the boyfriend had said in his interviews: his alibi, his whereabouts at the time of the crime, driving times and distances from the victim's home. All this resulted in pointing to a place where the body might be found. Did the detective relay this to Cynthia telepathically because he actually knew it subconsciously? Did she sense psychic information from the victim who needed her murder to be solved? Or from the murderer? Or from the collective universe?

"What do you think?" I asked, but before she could answer, Mae smiled, "Does it really matter? Probably the murder would never have been solved if it hadn't been for Cynthia."

Kait—A Murder Predicted

In their co-authored book *Psychic Connections: A Journey into the Mysterious World of Psi*, Lois Duncan and William Roll write about Lois's predictive experience. Lois had discovered that a number of details relating to the murder of her daughter Kait were things she had written about in her teenage suspense novel, *Don't Look Behind You*. The novel was published a month before Kait's death. It included the name of the man who would later be arrested for shooting Kait. Roll, who is the past president of the Oxford University Society for Psychical Research, commented, "Psychic bonds are not limited to people and things that are close to us in space and time, but include people and places far distant. To the psychic, out of sight does not mean out of mind."

Other Psychic Detectives

Trial lawyers in recent years have added psychics to their jury selection teams in an effort to determine whether prospective jurors are telling the truth. Also, a number of police agencies seemingly have benefited from assistance from so-called psychic detectives such as Greta Alexander of Delavon, Illinois Dorothy Allison of Nutley, New Jersey and John Catchings of Dallas.

CIA and the Soviets

In the past our government has indicated that it was interested in exploring the uses of extrasensory perception and other psychic phenomena as spy tools. In the 1960s the French magazine *Science et Vie* reported that the U.S. government had been successful in sending and receiving telepathic messages. According to this article, images were being telepathically transmitted from a laboratory near Baltimore to the submarine *Nautilus,* submerged at sea in the Atlantic. The author later said he discovered the story was a hoax and the United States denied the story. But this denial only convinced the Soviets that the U.S. might be on to something, that the denial was merely an attempt to throw them off. A Soviet scientist who had been quietly researching telepathy since the 1920s saw this as an opportunity, because the Marxist regime had viewed anything having to do with psychic powers as being counterrevolutionary.

Based on the belief that the French article was authentic, the Marxists now granted the scientist official approval to head a special parapsychology laboratory for telepathic investigations. Small leaks about this work began to appear, and the race was on, fueled in part by a book titled *Psychic Discoveries Behind the Iron Curtain,* by Sheila Ostrander and Lynn Schroeder, which claimed that the U.S. was fifty years behind the Russians in psychic research. Perhaps because of the news leaks that resulted from this book, Soviet parapsychology research was said to have been stopped. But our government's belief in the continuation of the Soviet ongoing research continued.

Our Government's Stargate

Meanwhile, our government learned in the 1970s that the Soviet Union was possibly experimenting with more than telepathy: It was said to be working with extrasensory perception, with the U.S. as its target. The Central Intelligence Agency perceived this possible threat to our national security as something that should be investigated in case the Soviets were right. believing that there could be some useful potential to ESP, the U.S. government began their own psychic research programs. One such psychic espionage operation—code-named "Stargate"—tried using psychics to discover the whereabouts of Libyan strongman "Muammar al-Khadafy in 1986, to seek plutonium in North Korea in 1994, to help out in the war on drugs, and other aborted missions.

In the summer of 1995, Congress commissioned the American Institute for Research to review Stargate and evaluate the effectiveness of this ESP espionage. One of two scientists, Jessica Utts, a statistics professor at the University of California at Davis, concluded that the case for psychic functioning has been scientifically proven. But University of Oregon psychology Professor Ray Hayman noted: "None of those psychics did a bit of good for the government."

Our government spent twenty years and $20 million to reach these opposing conclusions before the project was discontinued. All they discovered was that psychic energy, at least in their own programs, was an axion—that is, it could neither be proved or disproved.

However, former Army Captain David Morehouse, who developed his talents after a wartime injury released his latent psychic abilities, maintains that he was recruited into this clan of top secret psychic spies and discovered it was the plan of the CIA and the Defense Intelligence Agency to "take remote viewing to the realm of weaponry." In his book, *Psychic Warrior*, Morehouse, claims that he had powerful visions and dreams and participated in remote viewing sessions in which he felt as if he had actually gone to these locations. Determined to prevent his psychic powers from being used as a instrument of war, he embarked on a campaign to blow the lid off the top secret program. He worried about the use of his abilities to access thoughts in the minds of other human beings; his experiences took a tremendous emotional toll on him. Ultimately he was court-martialed and forced to resign. "It is chilling the lengths certain factions of the U.S. Government will go to hide the truth," he reports.

Psychic Survival

At the opposite end of the spectrum of huge governmental psychic projects and the use of psychic power in solving serious and major crime is the possibility that you can use your psychic powers to protect yourself from becoming a victim. In Gavin De Becker's book *The Gift of Fear—Survival Signals That Protect Us From Violence,* he tells a number of stories about how your own inner sense can help you avoid becoming a victim of crime. He relates the tale of a young woman named Kelly, who ignored at least five or six small details about her interaction with a stranger. She was picking up signals, being intuitively warned that he was dangerous, and any one of several clues should have alerted her, but she pushed these signals away as soon as they arose.

The stranger helped Kelly pick up her groceries when one of the bags she was carrying ripped. She ended up becoming his victim in a three-hour ordeal from which she was lucky to escape alive. She had heard no doors opening before the man appeared in the lobby of her building, she never heard the buzzer that would indicate one of her neighbors had let him in. She never questioned why he was going to the same floor as she was. She didn't question why this stranger was trying to charm her, helping her when she hadn't asked for help. He kept talking as they walked together toward her apartment, telling her details about himself, distracting her, telling her about his cat, why he was always late, providing disarming information about himself she hadn't requested. He promised to just put her groceries inside her apartment, being far too helpful, and when she said that wasn't necessary, he ignored her and she politely accepted help she didn't really need or want. Any one of the clues she got should have warned her that something was wrong. But they were small clues, not the kind of things you ordinarily pay attention to when you meet a smiling friendly person in the hallway of your apartment building—unless you have trained yourself to be observant, to be aware of energy projections, to respond when you get a gut reaction or when the image before you is somehow wrong. She not only chose to ignore them, she pushed them out of her consciousness because she had been taught to be nice, to be polite, to avoid offending, even total strangers. Kelly's layers of civilization prevented her from accessing her sixth sense, her intuition. Focusing on even one of these very subtle individual elements could have saved Kelly from a brutal experience. Although De Becker uses intuition in a very specialized sense, calling it "the gift of a brilliant internal guardian," it is the kind of focusing, concentration and attention to very minute detail that the psychic individual has. This is the kind of intuition about people and places which will bring warnings of hazards and guide you through risky situations. "Americans worship logic, even when it's wrong, and deny intuition, even when it's right," says De Becker.

Lola and the Protective Shield

Day-to-day living can be hazardous. A psychic shield can be added insurance and protection.

Lola, who had been in touch with her psychic powers through-out her life, says that she always uses a protective psychic shield to guard and insulate and protect herself and her family. "It only takes a few minutes to put one up and I do it daily. It's jut a little ritual," she said, "and anyone can do it." Lola nodded vigorously for emphasis. "I think it one of the most important things anyone who believes in energy fields can do. It protects you psychically and it makes you aware of the potential for danger, so that you are sort of a mental kung fu master of yourself before you leave your house every day."

Lola agreed to demonstrate her protective shield saying, "I look upon it as a short meditation, or some people might call it a prayer." She sat in front of me to demonstrate.

"I close my eyes and relax, but only for a moment. Then I visualize my bubble, this time a brilliantly white bubble, above my head and connected to my seventh chakra. I see my children and husband at my side and then I mentally put my arms around them. I bring the bubble down around all of us. I say, 'Repel all negative energy, protect and guide us throughout the day.' Then I just open my eyes. That's all there is to it." Lola's eyes sparkled and she smiled. "That's it! It doesn't require a long ritual or a lot of magic mumbo-jumbo, it's very straightforward. I'm happy with it and it serves me and my family well. Sometimes when I am under a lot of stress or there is a difficult situation facing one of us, such as a dental appointment, a difficult class assignment due, a rattle in the car that I don't know what the cause might be, I request protection and guidance. I will visualize it again during the day, just as a kind of reinforcement. My children love it, particularly my youngest. They all say it helps them to feel safe. They know I am with them, looking out for them."

"Couldn't that be dangerous?" I asked.

"Oh, no. It doesn't make them do foolish things. They know they still have to be careful. It is just a little bonus, like putting a note in their lunch box that says I'm thinking of them in a very positive way."

Suzy and the Ghost at the Side of the Road

Ross, a California forest ranger, was on duty in Yosemite National Park in California. "A young couple came to the ranger station just after dusk with what I thought was a wild, wild tale. The wife was pretty excited but the husband seemed to be a little embarrassed. Usually I get reports of bears in campsites or lost hikers but she had the kind of story I had never heard before. They told me they were on a climbing excursion in the park and as recreational climbers it was their intention to practice for an eventual climb of Mount Whitney. Although it was late evening when they finished setting up their tent at their campsite, they got back in their car to drive around and familiarize themselves with the area. It had suddenly gotten quite dark, as it can in the mountains, and there were no lights except from their headlights. They were feeling great, singing old camp songs they both remembered from childhood camping trips and ready to tackle some great climbs. Suddenly, at the side of the road where the road curves alongside a huge boulder, the wife, Suzy, saw a man lying there wearing one of those Tyrolian hats with a feather in it like they wear in the Alps. She told her husband Jeff to stop, but he the thought anyone out on the road at night might be dangerous. Besides, he told me, he thought was just her imagination. Suzy was adamant about having seen the man. She thought he was probably hurt, so Jeff drove to the ranger's station so she could report to me what she had seen."

Ross continued, "I went right out to the area of the big boulder but I didn't see anything. However, because they seemed like a sensible young couple I went back up as soon as it got light to look around again.

"I didn't see any man in an Alpine climber's outfit, but I did find a little Beanie Baby, you know one of those tiny toys that are so popular with the kids. Because of that, I decided to explore a little farther. I climbed down into a ravine and there I found a wrecked car with a man and a little girl in it! What none of us knew at the time was that this man had weekend custody of his three-year-old daughter and they both had been missing for almost a week. The child's mother thought her ex-husband had kidnapped their daughter and she had reported him to the police.

"As soon as I saw the man I knew he was dead. The car had crashed headlong into a tree and the steering wheel was crumpled into his chest. I assumed the little girl was dead too, but when I touched her she moved slightly. My hands were shaking when I radioed for an ambulance! I got a search crew out there too and we looked for several days to see if we could find that other man, the one Suzy saw lying at the side of the road, but we never found another person, if there ever had been one." Ross shook his head in wonder as he thought back to that day. "The temperature can get extreme during the night and I have no idea how that child survived. The pathologist said the father had been killed instantly and had been dead for about five days. The little girl, Robin, had just stayed by her father. She said later she tried to wake her daddy up but she couldn't. The doctor at the emergency room said the child couldn't have survived much longer without food or water in those nighttime temperatures."

Robin's mother is extremely grateful to Suzy and Jeff, but none of them has any idea who the man in the Tyrolian hat at the side of the road might have been. There had been no one else in the car when the father left with the little girl. "A hitchhiker? A ghost? Does it really matter?" asked Ross. "Being a forest ranger I find lots of things up here in the mountains are very wonderful and often unexplainable. I just accept that this happened. A child's life was saved by mysterious forces and I let it go at that."

Suzy's paranormal experience is one where the exact spot of an accident was pinpointed, making it easy for police and rescuers to find. But very often the information is vague and not understandable until much later.

You as a Psychic Detective

If you get a premonition when you see the report of a missing child on television or read about a crime in the paper—wait. Write down the your feelings and thoughts. Record the ideas you have about where the child might be found or who might have committed the murder. Follow the developments of the cases as they are revealed by the media and compare them with your impressions. Find out just how accurate you are. It is tempting to call the police, send them off in the direction you think they should be going— but what if you are wrong? That is an awesome responsibility.

If, after you have explored your psychic abilities on a dozen or more cases in which you can accurately document that the information you saw would have either found the child earlier or solved the crime sooner, then perhaps you are now in a position to offer your services to the authorities.

Perhaps you can become a famous psychic, assisting the police or appearing on television, although very few do. However, if you can protect yourself and your loved ones with the help of that universe of energy, that just might be enough.

EIGHT

Schemers, Scammers and Scoundrels: How Can You Avoid the Film-Flammers?

Mere film-flam stories, and nothing but shams and lies.
—Miguel de Cervantes in *Don Quixote*

There has always been controversy about whether or not psychics are, in fact, *real*. In the last century illusionists, mentalists, escape artists, conjurers and professional magicians have performed feats that seem magical and otherworldly to a naïve public.

One of the best known was the magician, mentalist and escape artist Harry Houdini, who, in the 1890s, transmitted coded signals to his wife by wiggling his ear, unobserved by his audience. Thus he was able to put on a impressive display of mind reading, or telepathy, then known as mentalism.

Theatrics and drama have always been a very large part of the presentations of these performers. They were entertainers, and as such they created a performance that would be dramatic, exciting and memorable. One well-known mentalist chewed on a piece of soap and claimed he was foaming at the mouth when he went into his trance. It had a powerful effect on his audience; people gasped at the sight. Dozens of other mentalists performed under the big top, with traveling circuses and carnivals big and small, and on stage in music halls and variety shows. Many were gifted magicians, and often used see-through blindfolds in their acts. All of them displayed their so-called talents for money. There have been psychic horses, geese and goats—today it is even possible to communicate with a psychic chicken on the Internet.

Another famous mentalist was six-foot tall Joseph Dunninger, who performed in the early 1900s. He read people's minds first on the stage and then on the radio, where he claimed he could read their minds over the air waves. He later appeared on television, where his thick black hair, mesmerizing stare, white gloves and matching spats, all served to enhance his dramatic image.

Dunninger was followed by the Great Kreskin who, as a child, had been fascinated by the comic-book character known as *Mandrake the Magician*. Kreskin appeared on stage as a hypnotist before he was in his teens, and by the 1960s he was a frequent guest on television variety shows, eventually moving on to have his own program. When questioned about his powers, Kreskin always replied that he didn't know how he came to have them. Amazingly, he never actually claimed to be psychic.

In the 1970s, Israeli Uri Geller performed amazing feats of psychokenetic strength by bending spoons, keys and other metal objects. Geller also claimed to have performed a form of aerial dowsing from an airplane. He wasn't looking for water; he was locating rich oil and diamond deposits for major companies. Geller's life story is told in the movie *Mindbender*.

James (The Amazing) Randi, a magician, has made a career out of the debunking of psychics worldwide, claiming that they are nothing more than skilled magicians. Randi routinely offers a huge reward to anyone who can prove, to *his* satisfaction, that they are psychic. To date no one has collected his reward money.

The Paranormal and Spirituality

There are those who connect the paranormal, including psychic abilities, to spirituality or religious practices. They view believers in psychic ability as being New Age searchers for a metaphysical meaning to their lives, because known religions have failed them. Many people in the 1970s became involved in so-called human potential movements, attending workshops, seminars and lectures in the hope of developing spirituality when religion no longer seemed to provide the comfort they needed. Many of the adherents of these movements expected that attaining psychic powers would be a natural byproduct of this quest.

Others are fearful of the paranormal, and some religions prohibit the use of tarot cards, Ouija boards, astrological charts and other means of seeing into the future, suggesting that they are in some fashion connected to Satanism or devil worship.

For some the paranormal connects with powerful emotional needs that scientific explanations of the workings of the universe leave unfulfilled. A belief in the paranormal appears to respond to deep spiritual hunger, to the need to find cures for disease, for all kinds of instant magic or miracles in otherwise routine and hum-drum lives. Belief in reincarnation, ghosts, and the channeling of entities who lived thousands of years ago all appear to promise that death is not the end. Such belief affirms that we are hooked up with and firmly connected to the Universe—that life is not finite but infinite, and we are central to the cosmos. Sometimes it appears to serve as a kind of halfway house between old religion and new science and affirms that our lives are important.

Perhaps we need to accept that there is a great need for the very things that acceptance of the reality of the paranormal might bring to our lives. It is detrimental to the completeness of our lives to deny its power.

Channeling

Currently, channeling appears to have replaced mediums—those who spoke for the dead or other entities in seances—as the New Age venue for communications with either the dead or entities of all types, such as those who purportedly now live on other planets or in other worlds. One of the best known is Ramtha, the 35,000-year-old warrior from the lost continent of Atlantis who is channeled through J. Z. Knight. In a theatrical display J.Z. is garbed in a flowing robe and sits on a dais high above her enthralled followers and speaks in the voice of Ramtha. Ramtha's message is simple: We all bear God within ourselves, right or wrong is determined by the individual. Ramtha also says each of us has the power and the will to control our own destiny. This positive, uplifting, and fairly commonsense message has earned Ms. Knight millions.

The World

In Algeria more and more people are discreetly consulting the country's 10,000 soothsayers and clairvoyants (about half of whom operate with a license from the government). In Germany, dangerous "earth rays" are being hunted by experienced dowsers. Psychic surgery flourishes in the Philippines and ghosts are something of a national obsession in Britain. An estimated 100,000 fortune-tellers are at work in Japan and thousands of people attend a pagan spirit gathering annually in the U.S. The worldwide transcendental meditation (TM) organization has an estimated value of $3 billion. It is obvious that there is a worldwide hunger to contact the paranormal in one manner or another.

Psychic Hotlines

In the U.S., hundreds of thousands of people call psychic hotlines in response to very persuasive television commercials, those infomercials that run twenty-four hours a day on almost every channel. *Insights on the News* magazine reported in 1996 that The Psychic Friends Network's television infomercials earn approximately $1.5 million a week and have attracted over ten million calls. The average call costs $40—and that's just one of the dozens of such psychic hotlines that are on the air. With such potential earning power, it is no wonder that these psychic phone lines have proliferated.

Two young women, recently profiled on *NBC Nightly News* with Tom Brokaw, detailed their need to call a such a psychic hotline daily. The women were at a loss to know how they were going to pay their $4,000 telephone bill.

Police routinely are called upon to investigate fortune-tellers who advertise in the Yellow Pages, or crystal ball gazers who run storefront operations with blinking neon signs advertising their help to anyone who wishes to stop by. It is easy for the unscrupulous to set up shop and scam the gullible and psychologically needy. Rational individuals have given a fortune-teller hundreds of thousands of dollars, sometimes their life's savings, for their help in communicating with the dead, lifting a curse, curing a disease, finding the right loving mate, providing a winning lottery number, or picking the name of a winner in an upcoming horse race.

Just who are these people who earn a living in this way?

I decided to check out some of the psychic products available to the average consumer. After consulting the Yellow Pages and my local newspaper I was able to locate some in my community. I paid $100 an hour to a well-dressed Englishwoman, a tarotologist, who told me she was the foremost expert on the subject. I had an entertaining afternoon and was told that I could move if I wished to. I would have spent about the same for an evening at the theater in New York City. I visited a crystal ball gazer dressed in blue jeans whose children played at her feet as she told me how many children I had—information I already knew, of course, but it was fun to see if she was accurate. Later I had my palm read at a carnival by a woman decked out in the requisite gold hoop earrings and was told I would live a long life. What a relief. I spent a few minutes with someone with a foreign accent on a psychic hotline. We did not get around to a reading because when I asked about the baby I could hear crying in the background, I was told there was no baby, I must be hearing angels. I had my astrological chart done by an expert I met at a New Age bookstore, and by a computer. I learned from the expert that I am creative and interesting, that people like me, and that I might take a trip soon. Who would deny being creative and interesting? Who wants to think that they aren't likable and yes, I did take a short trip thereafter. I went to spiritualists and received messages from my father and from a favorite cat. They both told me to behave myself. Pretty good advice.

I do not doubt that some of these individuals were sincere, some were just making a living, and some were both. It is up to me to decide which was which and whether or not to follow any advice given. Fortunately I was not given any drastic advice, such to quit my job, move to Beirut or to marry the next tall dark stranger that I might meet. I have at least tried to follow the advice given by both my deceased father and my long-dead but beloved cat Sidney.

In my search for one of the psychics who actually work at a hot line I met Val, a pleasant young woman who is now working as a waitress. She readily agreed to talk with me about her experiences working as a telephone psychic.

"How did you get the job?" I asked

"I was looking in the Help Wanted section in the Sunday paper and I saw an ad: 'Work out of your home, no selling,' and the pay was $12 an hour. It sounded pretty good to a waitress who is used to getting minimum wage plus tips. I have small children and I would love to be able to stay at home with them. It sounded wonderful to me," she replied with a smile. "The training was quick and simple—about twenty minutes. I was told to get the caller's birthday first, then give them a little horoscope reading out of a standard astrology book which the company supplied. Not only was that a kind of warm-up, but it kept the caller on the line longer—often they replied to the astrology information and, although they often didn't realize it, their responses gave me useful information. If they were young, I was told they would want advice about 'money and a honey' and an older person would be interested in 'health and wealth.' Of course, getting their birth date gave me the answer to their age from the very start." Val continued, "I was given a deck of tarot cards and told to write a bunch of 'trigger' words on them, so that while I talked I could turn up the cards randomly and use them to help me think of what to say next. I had to develop a patter because, as I soon found out, that promised $12 an hour really meant only if I kept a customer on the line."

"You mean you didn't get $96 a day?" I said.

"Oh, no. I could sit home all day and not get a call transferred to me if other people had been better the day before at keeping the callers on the line. Some days I didn't earn a dime; and, if I didn't do well at keeping customers hooked, then I went to the bottom of the list for the next day."

"So what did you do?" I asked.

"Well," she said, "I learned real fast. I'd begin with that little astrology warm-up, describing the customer so they would believe that I was 'reading' them. I'd take my time with that, pumping up the minutes, especially if I got any responses that told me I was telling them what they wanted to hear."

"What was the horoscope like?" I asked.

"Well, think about the horoscope that's in the paper every day. It's written in generalities, stuff that anybody could think applies to them, particularly if they like it. You can throw in a little mystical astrological mumbo-jumbo stuff like, 'your sun is trine to Pluto, your Venus is square to Aquarius,' It made me sound like an expert. I was never caught by anyone who knew more about astrology than me. Next I might say, 'You have a fine sense of humor, but sometimes your little jokes are misunderstood. You are talented in an area where you seldom are given an opportunity to show what you can do. Your coworkers often don't appreciate you. You hide your sensitive nature so that your friends won't know how really insecure you feel. Friends think you are so confident, they sometimes wish they could be more like you. You are meticulous about your work but really dislike having to give so much attention to unimportant detail. You have an adventurous nature but never take really great risks. You could be a wonderful, loving partner if you could meet the person who comes up to your standards, but that is difficult to find today.' If I gave you that description of yourself, you'd probably agree, right?"

"Yes, of course," I answered.

"You see," Val said, "it is so ambiguous it could really apply to anybody. Nobody thinks of themselves as humorless, insensitive, boring. It is general and flattering and the caller actually ends up interpreting what I have said as being a customized revelation about themselves. During that patter the clients usually responded to some of the statements and give me clues they didn't even realize they were giving me. I asked very general questions such as, 'Have you ever thought about going into business for yourself?' or 'Do find that you are sometimes thinking about someone from your past?' I would be as amazed as they were when they thought these questions were insightful, because I would think everyone, at some time in their lives, has given some thought to going into business for themselves, or about some person from their past. As soon as they started to talk, I just listened. They ended up being amazed at how 'psychic' I was. And they spent some real money!"

"So if it's so easy, why you aren't doing it anymore?" I asked. I could tell she was embarrassed.

She looked away for a moment before she answered. "I earned more money than some of my friends because I have a pretty good gift of gab," she said. "But I just felt terrible. I'm not psychic. I was giving complete strangers a line of bull, telling them stuff that might affect their lives, and keeping them on the phone for my benefit, not theirs. I just couldn't do it any longer, but lots of others can. Perhaps some of them really are psychic, I can't really know. It's pretty good money and sometimes both you and the caller have a lot of fun but most of the others I knew were just there for the money."

"What happens if people complain?" I asked.

"Look on the bottom of the TV screen when commercials come on. You will see the disclaimer, 'For entertainment only,' and that's what it is supposed to be, entertainment. That disclaimer legally protects the company," she answered.

The Psychic Friends Network recently filed for bankrupcy, claiming an indebtedness of $25 million. If anyone doubts that psychic hotlines are not the best way to contact the paranormal, the fact that 2,000 alleged psychics employed by this hotline apparently did not "see" this coming should speak for itself.

My mother frequently was sought out by people who wanted advice, not a connection to the paranormal. Often they would have their tea leaves read five or six times before they would ask: "What do you think I should do?" "Will I ever get married?" "Should I change jobs?" It didn't take Mae long to see that they were looking for a counselor, not a psychic. She would gently suggest that they seek the help of someone whose business was to advise people— a psychologist, a marriage counselor, a spiritual advisor. She was firm in her belief that it was her task to connect to the paranormal for them and then turn the impressions she received into words. But the interpretation was up to them.

Psychic healing

Healing is an important topic when it comes to the psychic, because its misuse can be life threatening. This is particularly true if the individual delays or avoids seeking other help, relying solely on psychic healing and thus allowing the disease process to become advanced.

The medicine man, medicine woman or shaman is a religious specialist in some nonwestern cultures and their main function is to cure disease. The healing powers of these individuals are based on the culturally accepted assumption that most, if not all, illnesses are caused by some supernatural power, and that supernatural powers are required for a cure. The patient may fall ill for offending one of the gods, through the machinations of witchcraft or sorcery, or through the unprovoked attack of an evil spirit. The task of the medicine man and medicine woman is to diagnose the disease, and then to apply the spiritual remedy, such as retrieving a lost soul, removing a disease-causing object, or exorcising an evil spirit. During the course of this ritual healing, which can often take days, these healers may also employ physical remedies such as herbs or magic potions.

Anthropologists have observed that frequently the medicine man or medicine woman benefits the patient. This may be because that particular culture supports belief in the ritual. Or the medicine man or medicine woman may actually have knowledge of the curative value of herbs. Also, many illnesses have psychological causes, and the shaman's ritual can provide a psychological release.

Psychic surgery is widely practiced in the Philippines by so-called "surgeons" who make a dramatic performance out of "balancing magnetic forces" and by massage with oil and holy water. Most of these alleged healers have no interest in the so-called paranormal—they are simply con artists taking advantage of the neediest and most frightened people—those who are looking for a miracle to save their lives. Investigators have observed how, by folding their fingers under as they massage the client's belly, it is made to appear that they have nonsurgically entered the abdomen of the patient. With a magician's sleight-of-hand, such performing "surgeons" appear to remove tumors—actually cut-up pieces of chicken intestine they have hidden up their sleeve. They also flood the surgical area with blood from a secreted vial of cow's blood. Investigators have brought back samples of waste from some of these psychic surgeries, had it analyzed at reputable laboratories, and found absolutely no human tissue or blood in the samples.

Thousands of people ignore or discontinue legitimate treatment in order to take advantage of psychic surgery or the latest in fashionable miracles. And they sometimes die brutal, ugly deaths.

A very attractive young woman in a New Age shop handed me her business card. It had her phone number, her E-mail address, a seven-digit license number, and the statement, "Licensed Professional Psychic." It certainly gave the impression that she had credentials from the state of Florida and undoubtedly that was the impression she wished to create. After some checking I learned that in reality she is licensed to do business in the state, having paid the same fee for a business license as is granted to anyone who owns or operates a small business or a shop.

Perhaps a visit to a fortune-teller or a tarotologist for a reading might be fun. If that is all it is for you, then it is as harmless as spending the afternoon at the movies. But if you are like the hundreds of thousands of people who turn to complete strangers and ask them to make major decisions about their lives or expect a miracle cure, you had better remember: Let the buyer beware!

"There is no Better Business Bureau in the world of psychics."

Your Psychic Truth

As you listen to your psychic self, you will *know* what is psychically true. There will be a different kind of sense, a clarity, a rightness to the information you receive.

If you are doing a psychic reading for someone else, you should not interpret the message for them. For example, if you, as a psychic, tell them you see a pony, it will have no meaning to you because you cannot know what a pony means in their lives. But they may understand the significance of the pony. Symbols are the language of the collective unconscious speaking directly to the subconscious. Through the use of symbols the etheric message is made concrete.

Ultimately, a sincere psychic will not give advice but will only give information that each person can interpret based on the meaning of the symbols they have seen or dreamed. When the symbol is so subtle that it does not readily elicit a response, some simple questions should be asked: How does this symbol make you feel? What past experiences or associations are connected to this symbol? Free association can often bring clarity.

How can you avoid being scammed?

*Learn to access and trust **your own** sixth sense.*

NINE

Let's Give Mom the Winning Lottery Number: What's Wrong With That?

Mr. Turnbull had predicted evil consequences . . . and now was doing the best in his power to bring about the verification of his own prophecies.

—Anthony Trollope, *Phineas Finn*

Our modern world has great difficulty accepting, believing in, or even honoring the honesty of those who say they see the supposedly invisible. It is simple to deal with what is plainly and clearly before us, but the world appears to have forgotten how to see what is now hidden under the huge technological glut of modern living. If you have read this far, practiced the exercises, and kept a dream journal, you surely have already proven to yourself that your own connection to the psychic realm is possible and real. You have found your psychic self. Perhaps you have had no more than a subtle feeling, a sudden change of mood which was unexplained. But now there is an explanation. You have received a message from the universal consciousness. Maybe a currently troubling problem, something you had been worried about for quite some time, is now clear and resolved. With just a little effort in relearning how to make that connection to the paranormal, it has broken through to you.

Perhaps you have had an even stronger signal that the world of your sixth sense is real. Maybe you have had a telepathic communication, a prophetic dream, or a strong experience of déjà vu. Such an experience is proof that you are on the way to rediscovering that skill you once had, but long since lost or forgot you ever knew.

Perhaps recently you have been struggling with a decision— whether to trust someone, the correct solution to an important business decision, how to determine if a new project is good for you; or perhaps you have been hesitant about embarking upon a different course when the future of that choice is mysterious, frightening, maybe even dangerous. If you have been practicing connecting with your psychic self, you can now accept that you can directly receive your own psychic guidance. Now, despite what others may have suggested you should do—well-meaning advice that perhaps is not in your best interest—your psychic connection can provide the right information to guide you.

If you have suddenly awakened in the morning with the solution to a weighty problem firmly in your mind, you know that your psychic abilities are working. Possibly a dream has given you the answer you were seeking. If this has happened and you have relied on your own intuition, you have now rediscovered and connected with your own psychic abilities. Now you can experience the sense of joy that comes with such self-proof of the reality of your sixth sense.

Mae's Psychic Gift

When Mae was a very young woman, she was often sought by others because of her psychic gifts. She soon learned that it was best never to give advice, but rather to tell people what she saw and let each person interpret the images or dreams she had for or about them. As she matured, she became even more cautious, doing what she called a psychic scanning, by taking the person's hand, listening to their voice with her eyes closed, feeling their energy, before she would agree to read their tea leaves. In later years Mae spent much more time teaching others how to connect with their own psychic sense. She made the learning fun, with things like the plant exercise, allowing people to easily experience their own power, rather than connecting for them. She believed that everyone could relearn how to find their own psychic abilities, and that everyone should.

She was often asked if she thought some people could become psychic more quickly than others and just what it felt like to be psychic. Her answer was, "Psychic experiences are very emotional. Someone who is already generous with their time, their heart, who is empathetic, is more likely to access and accept the images and the emotions that flow with those images. They will accept and understand easily that they come from the paranormal. But if your life experiences have taught you to be tight and constricted emotionally, it will take a little longer to unlearn those limitations. But I believe everyone can relearn what they knew as children and learn to be psychic again."

If you are someone who opens up easily to intuitive experiences and recognizes them when they happen, you can probably easily relearn your psychic abilities. If you already enjoy the feeling of silk clothing against your skin, if you impulsively bring home a bouquet of flowers just because the colors caught your eye as you passed by, it will be easier for you to reclaim your sixth sense. If you perfume the air in your house, listen to beautiful music and take the time to hear what children have to say, it will be easier for you to recover your psychic skills. If you stop to pet a stranger's dog on the street corner, frequently look up at the sky to watch a bird soaring overhead, you can quickly restore your connection with the paranormal. If you enjoy good food beautifully presented and like to take a walk in the quiet of the evening just to admire the sunset, you probably are very psychic. If you have good warm friendships and love to spend time with those friends—laughing, talking, crying, sharing their lives—you probably are well aware that you are psychic, because psychics are sensuous people.

Psychics are seldom lonely or separated or isolated from others. They are aware of the world around them, happy in their relationships with people and nature. Some people, of course, are already psychic; they know and accept their experiences with the paranormal because they understand that the experience is just another example of their interconnectedness with the universe. They understand that there are no boundaries between the individual and the universal consciousness, that it is available instantly to anyone who is in that altered state of consciousness that comes from meditating and being very relaxed. With just a little bit of effort, almost everyone who desires to do so can connect with the paranormal.

It was obvious to everyone who knew her that my mother was one of the sensuous people. Curious about everything and everyone, enthusiastic about life, she treasured the friendship of many, some she had known her entire life, and truly enjoyed meeting new people. She had an adventurous soul and I would often come home to find a professional wrestler, a hippie guru, the mailman, or the delivery boy from a local store, laughing and enjoying tea in our kitchen. She was gracious, generous, charming and very witty. She took everything in stride, every up or down, every twist and turn of life, and she laughed, danced, and sang along the way. She had that personal magnetism that attracted others, the human gift that is now often called charisma.

A very early memory of mine is of being awakened at dawn on the first of May so that we could go outside and wash our faces in the dew on the grass to ensure we would be beautiful all year long. As a grumpy, sleepy child I would reluctantly get up just before daylight but as we danced around a May pole she had made and decorated with long shiny satin ribbons in glorious colors, I would be laughing and happy. Another favorite memory is of dancing foursome and eightsome reels with both my parents at the St. Andrew's Society Hall, a Scottish social club. Children weren't left home, we were included in everything. While the adults talked we would slide on the slick wooden dance floor or run through the meeting rooms until the music started again. I felt safe and secure there, with a connectedness that comes with being included, a part of an intangible something larger than myself.

Scottish people love sing-a-longs; whether you can carry a tune or not doesn't matter. Some evenings at home Mae would play the piano and friends from what they called the auld country would sing songs that reminded them of a home that, at that moment, most of them thought they would never see again. Later, snug in my bed, between sleeping and dreaming, I would hear laughter floating back on the wind, and the sounds of accented Scottish voices calling out their goodnights to my mother as she stood in the doorway waving to the last visitors as they went down the front path.

Frequently, those she had taught, who had practiced and become far more intuitive than they ever imagined they could be, who had become friends during that journey, urged her to write a book about being psychic. She always said she planned to do it when she could get around to it, but she never did.

When Mae died, I was aware of what I have described as her energy around me for several days, and it was comforting. Now, years later, I often feel as if she is in the room, and I have found myself looking around to see if she is there. But of course she isn't. This is an experience I share with millions of others who have lost a loved one. Many cultures delay burial for three days, understanding this energy transfer far better than our very civilized world does today. They allows time for the person's energy to leave the earthly body and join the collective or universal consciousness. I have spoken to many people who have experienced this after-death energy. No one spoke of ghosts or feeling haunted, but of being strongly aware of the person's presence around them for a few days.

Some time after she died, I had a very vivid dream about my mother Mae. She was smiling at me and nodding her head. She didn't speak, and when I woke up I lay very still for a few moments, trying to gather together the fragments of that dream. I was happy to have dreamed that she was smiling at me, obviously approving of something. It was the memory of this dream that caused me to begin jotting down notes about everything I could recall she had ever said about learning to be psychic, or what it felt like to be psychic. I remembered the many workshops, classes and seminars we had gone to and the things we had learned there. That remembered dream was the beginning of this book.

Trying to explain the experience of the paranormal to those who are doubtful of its existence is always very difficult. I find myself using struggling to find the right descriptive terms that can convey the feeling of enchantment or joy that experiencing this connection to the universe brings, without sounding pretentious. Watching someone's world expand to include the reality of the psychic realm is like watching a child open gifts on Christmas morning, opening the door to a universe of wonder. This is a universe that was there all the time, only just beyond reach.

Once you have experienced it for yourself it will resonate with truth, you will feel a joyous rapture in being alive. Rediscovering and knowing your sixth sense will enrich your life. Once you experience it you will have a feeling of supreme well-being, perhaps like the child that is deep down inside you, jumping into the pool on a summer's day, or kicking your feet up to the clouds as you were pushed on a swing in the playground, feelings you had forgotten or maybe you didn't know were possible any longer. You will discover that reclaiming your psychic self and finding the psychic realm a life-altering and life-enhancing experience, one that is but a few deep breaths away.

One caution however: psychic experiences, whatever joy and enchantment they bring, are transitory. You need to be well grounded so that you do not get blown away by gales of emotion or lost in the experience, because the psychic person is someone who also easily opens up to emotion.

There are always some who think being psychic or intuitive is in some way mystical or supernatural, associated with religion or superstition. It is a very natural skill or talent, one everyone can reclaim. I don't recall that my mother read or talked about quantum physics, although I would not have been surprised if she had, but her ideas about the universe were very much like those of physicist David Bohm, whose thinking treated the totality of existence, including matter and consciousness, as an unbroken whole. He rejected a mechanistic world, one in which matter and consciousness are outside of each other and exist independently—the world as described by Sr. Isaac Newton. Bohm spoke of an enfolding-unfolding universe in which everything existed in a state of undivided flowing movement, energy without borders, and I think Mae would have loved that description.

Stanford's William Tiller, in his preface to Bentov's *Stalking the Wild Pendulum*, wrote, "There have been small beginnings made toward a new self-image for humankind, one that emphasizes the human wholeness and connectivity with everything around it. Everything seems to interact with everything else at many subtle levels of the universe beyond the purely physical level, and the deeper we penetrate into these other levels, the more we realize that we are One."

I taken part in many conversations over the years about the religious aspects of the paranormal or supernatural, and I always find the example of electricity a good allegory. Although it sounds simplistic, it was usually effective. If asked, "How do you think electricity works?" most of us really don't know, including me. Most people explain it simply by saying, "I don't know, some kind of energy comes through wires in the house and lights the lamp and runs the washing machine." And they are usually joined in laughter at their description.

There is seldom any disagreement about the fact that electricity is "some kind of energy." When questioned further, few people think electricity or the energy that produces it, is religious, they think it is just *there*, and anyone can choose to turn the light on or run the washing machine. In fact, most people laugh at the idea of electricity being in any way a religious phenomenon. However, electricity can be used by people for a variety of purposes. If you don't believe in capital punishment, then using electricity to power the electric chair is an evil use; if you use electricity to light up the scene of a nighttime accident so people can be rescued, then it is a good use.

If you can separate the universe from a spiritual or religious concept, perhaps you can accept that the universe is made up of energy fields that are in an unending process of interacting and converging into infinity. However, if the universe and its behavior isn't spiritual, if the universe just *is,* there cannot be a spiritual or religious aspect to the use of psychic consciousness. So, if it pleases you to make your connection with the paranormal part of a religious or spiritual experience, you probably should, because that will be beneficial to you and it can enhance your spiritual quest.

For anyone who is concerned about connecting with psychic energy means that you are involved with the occult, you can call your intuitive experiences "mere coincidences."

I recall listening to Mae and her good friend Violet, a professional translator whose original language was Hungarian but who spoke and read six or seven other languages, and who loved to have her tea leaves read. Violet worried about the fact that her church would never approve of talking about the paranormal or trying to contact other realms.

Violet said, "I worry about the 'huge web of the universe' and energy fields, and I imagine it as a gigantic spider web, with threads criss-crossing each other and interlocking. It seems very different from a universe in which there are places such as heaven and hell, with punishment or rewards in a life hereafter for being bad or good."

Mae always took Violet's concerns seriously. But she thought that any psychic, aware of the interconnectedness of the universe would do nothing but treat themselves, others, animals, and the earth with respect because they are all connected. She said, "That has everything or nothing to do with religion. We are talking about energy fields, not right or wrong."

Imagine a universe that is separate from the beliefs and practices of any religion, not limited by a particular religion's concepts. Consider it a continuously flowing and interlocking energy-fields-universe. You will come to understand that it is what people DO with the energy that makes the difference.

If you are willing to accept the concept of waves of energy, in dynamic relationships to each other, then you will accept that the universe is like an ocean, and we are all swimming in those energy fields. If you happen to come in contact with a negative or detrimental person, you are perfectly justified in defending yourself against anyone who puts these energy fields to negative uses.

It is actually taking the concept the next step, to the behavior of humans, that gets into the realm of religion. Any religious person should have no difficulty in seeing that how you use or what you do with the universe's energy is the next step, the step into a religious or spiritual concept.

Many people ask for wisdom or psychic guidance. That can be called a prayer, if you wish. Asking that you will only get good information from the universal consciousness and use the information you receive for a higher purpose naturally should be a part of any psychic experience.

Violet was finally able to reconcile her religious beliefs with acceptance of the paranormal as part of her life, thanks to a philosophical discussion that went on for years. She and Mae talked about a lot of other topics, agreed and disagreed, argued and debated. Their friendship continued and deepened and was never harmed by the paranormal connection; it was only enriched by their conversations.

It is necessary to seek paranormal connection with empathy and compassion. You must open your heart to others to be a good psychic. You must grow personally so that you can tell the difference between that constant conversation with yourself that goes on in all of our minds and information from the paranormal that can only be heard if your mental static is silenced. Even if you are a well-grounded individual, you will experience a stream of emotion with each psychic experience as the information comes flowing in, sometimes completely structured and sometimes in fragmented concepts or symbolic pictures. Whether you are connecting in a reading for someone else or in finding your own answers, these emotions can be strong, even rapturous. Sometimes the images and the emotions they evoke are overwhelming, but once you have such an experience, nothing in your life is ever the same again.

I can remember Mae's admonition, "Be aware that there are responsibilities that come with the power to access your sixth sense and gain information from the universal consciousness."

To be psychic is to be responsible, to respect the boundaries of others, because with intuition must come commitment. You must commit yourself to being accurate, to being caring and wise with the use of the information you receive in this way. You need to practice receiving psychic guidance for yourself before you ever attempt to do so for any one else. And, if you choose to read someone's tea leaves, do a tarot spread, or look into a crystal ball for them, you must remember that you should never take away their personal power. They have asked you for psychic help because they want to get a clue to guide them in the right direction, sometimes in a major life altering decision. It is very easy to give advice but it is even easier to interpret the symbols inaccurately. *Always let the subject make their own interpretations.*

In *Man and his Symbols,* Jung tells us that each of us receives a notion in the context of our own individual mind, and we each therefore understand and apply an idea in our own way. Because no two life experiences have been identical, each word in the language means something different to each person, even among those who share the same cultural or family background. This is a most important point and even Jung, a psychoanalyst, admitted that he was incapable of interpreting symbols for patients. They had to interpret them for themselves.

King Croesus and the Oracle

It is important to look closely at the message and the person for whom the message is intended, to understand what the symbols in that message might mean.

* * *

If you misunderstand the message, it can have disastrous results.

King Croesus, who reigned about 560 B.C., was the last king of Lydia, an ancient country of Asia Minor. He increased his territories by conquest after conquest, winning a vast treasure that made his wealth so proverbial it gave rise to the adage, "as rich as Croesus."

According to legend, Croesus visited the Delphic oracle and was told that if he crossed the Halys River he would destroy a large kingdom. Of course, Croesus believed that he would enrich himself once again. But he was completely defeated in the battle. The meaning of the prediction was one he had not even considered: The kingdom he had destroyed was his own.

Twain and His Premonition

It is important also that, when you have a premonition, to consider whether or not it is prudent for you to pass that information along.

Mark Twain spent many years as a riverboat pilot on the Mississippi River. He had a dream that his brother Henry was a corpse lying in a metallic burial case in his sister's living room. When he awoke in the morning Twain told his sister of his nightmare. They were both horrified to learn, only a few weeks later, that Henry had died when his ship's boiler exploded.

What might have happened if Twain had told his brother of his dream? Predictive dreams are not absolute, they are only possibilities. Would Henry have quit the ship he was destined to die on and suffered a different fate? Perhaps that would have made no difference, he might have died in another accident somewhere else. And if Twain had told his brother of his dream, how would the universe have been altered if Henry had changed his life, because he still had free will, and affected the lives of others? We will never know, but these are philosophical and ethical questions to ponder when you think of telling others not what you see, but how you interpret what you see. Be careful of the choices you make for others.

Tony and the Bloody Hands

Tony had a dream and saw his mother with her hands over her face, crying, her hands covered in blood. Worried that his mother would be injured in an accident, he immediately called her and asked her to stay home, that he would come to her that day, rather than her visiting him. On his way to her house, the psychic had a terrible accident. When his mother learned of the accident and rushed to the scene, she held her injured son close to her as they waited for the ambulance. The blood he had seen on her hands turned out to be his, not his mother's. Tony had not been careful enough in his interpretation of this dream and what he did to alter the course of the future.

Kathy and Her Doubts

Mae's friend Kathy frequently had precognitive experiences. While she was quite comfortable in describing the energy fields she felt from others and the auras she frequently saw, she was still hesitant about relying on her psychic skills in her own life. Frequently she would tell Mae vivid details of her dreams, but would be at a loss to understand their meaning. Mae encouraged her to keep a dream journal, to try free association until the meaning of those symbols in her dreams became clear, and to learn to interpret her own dream symbolism. She asked her to make a record of the repeated symbolism she saw, to look for patterns and to record whether the dream was about the past, the present or the future. Kathy impatiently brushed away such suggestions.

"I just need to have a dream that will give me some lottery

numbers so I can win a lot of money. That would solve all my problems," Kathy often declared.

"I'm sure it would," laughed Mae, "but unfortunately, while I truly doubt that would solve all your problems, it doesn't seem to work like that for you or very many others."

"All I want are just a few little lottery numbers. That doesn't seem to be asking too much. I could give the numbers to my mother, then she would win the money and give some of it to me, so I wouldn't feel greedy or selfish," said Kathy crossly, ignoring Mae's words. "How about that woman who won millions in Las Vegas?" she would ask, "Why can't that happen to me?"

"You're not listening," answered Mae. "Psychic information often comes in symbols, or in feelings, or vague emotional sensations. The woman in Las Vegas had a premonition, a feeling that she should do something. She acted on it, immediately, because it felt so right to her. How often have you had such a feeling and then just dismissed it because it wasn't what you wanted to do at the moment? She paused. Kathy looked downcast because she knew there had been many times when she had ignored her intuition. "Only you can interpret those feelings, sensations, and symbols you receive in your dreams. The true secret to the joy and euphoria of the psychic world is just that—the feelings, the emotions, the sensations you experience. There is no greater feeling than to realize that you have understood, intuitively, at your gut level, when something is right and correct for you. You are in synchronization with the rhythm of the universe. That is worth more than any lottery number because it is the opportunity to feel really alive!"

Interpreting Symbols

Interpretation of the images and emotions that flow or the remembered fragments of dreams is an important aspect of understanding information from the psychic realm. If the psychic *interprets* what is seen for someone else, that interpretation can be fraught with danger. The psychic can be the vehicle for accessing the message but the interpretation of that message must absolutely must be left to the person for whom the message is intended. Because time can be altered in this dimension, visions are not always of the future. If the psychic decides to give advice or direct the life or future of another, it is possible that the interpretation of predictions can lead both the psychic and the listener in the wrong direction, and possibly to life-altering errors.

As a psychic it is possible to see a *probable* future occurrence, but not an *absolute* future occurrence. No matter what a psychic sees, each of us still has free will and can decide whether or not we want to act on the information.

We Need the Magic

What should be the purpose of opening yourself to this other dimension of time and space, this sixth sense? Why should you find your psychic self? You've been getting along just fine without it, or with only the barest flashes of the experience. Often, like a will-o'-the-wisp, no more than a vapor, an airy nothing, psychic experiences come and are gone. Why bother?

There is an important answer to that question, one that says that having and using your sixth sense is essential. *When you once experience the paranormal you will realize that you have been existing in a black-and-white world when all the time everything around you was really happening in technicolor!*

As our world has become more mechanistic and scientific, we have come to believe that science is some kind of power all its own. If science isn't involved in the study of something, if a scientist wearing a lab coat doesn't appear on television to proclaim something to be bona fide, backed up with reports of statistical possibilities and articles in serious journals, many of us have been taught, and have come to believe, that it can't be worthwhile or even real. We have moved away from the paranormal, rejected it just because it isn't scientific or because it appears to be connected to the mystical, the spiritual, the supernatural, or even the devil and the occult. We want to avoid being labeled some kind of a nut, a weirdo, or at the very least eccentric, by accepting and believing in something that, as yet, cannot be scientifically demonstrated to exist.

There is a movement at the moment to avoid the using the word "psychic," as if to say that you are psychic is to admit you are some kind of a New Age kook. Many are now using the word "intuitive" instead, trying to appear more scientific—the very thing that has taken the joy out of the paranormal. There are people who are now calling themselves "intuitive counselors," "intuitive trainers" and "seers." It isn't important what a psychic is called, these are just words that describe people who are enriching their lives.

It is because of science that we no longer believe in fire-breathing dragons or mermaids, and I miss them. Science appears to have taken the joy out of life by explaining away all the mystery and the magic. Science has brought us a world where everything is logical, demonstrable by repeatable scientific studies and it has, in many instances, created a dull and mundane place. Science's world is completely orderly instead of entertainingly chaotic. Missing in that monochromatic world are all those childish things that contribute to the creation of a total human being—one who is playful and joyous, who meets the new adventures that life brings with a delighted enthusiasm, while still being responsible and mature.

Mae and Delight in the Sixth Sense

Mae believed that as humans we need magic. We need to suddenly experience the unexpected, the surprises of life. It is because psychic power or intuition is so elusive and unprovable that it is delightful. Just like other surprises, the delight is often in the unexpected experience. When you need to know something, and suddenly a book on the topic appears in the mail from a friend, this synchronicity is more than just a casual event. Obviously, it is part of a plan. Being psychic opens you to another world, where synchronicity has meaning and that gives life another dimension, one of pleasure and enchantment."

Being psychic means that you experience strong emotions and handle them well. It means that you will have moments when your heart is brimming with love, when you are electrified by the beauty of a flower or a person, when you are overjoyed at the pleasure your dog takes in greeting you when you come through the door at the end of the day. It means that you can be transported to another dimension by the simple joy in the sound of a violin, your heart can resonate to the words in a song. It means that you can open a book of poetry and find words there that thrill your soul. This psychic sense, this sixth sense, can be added to the other five and its inclusion can heighten, deepen, intensify and enhance those others in exciting and creative ways. Being psychic can make your very existence rapturous, even ecstatic.

As you access your sixth sense, you become a person who knows how to tune in to a voice that comes simultaneously from deep within yourself and at the same time from the vortex of the energy of the universe. These voices join to give you an intuitive truth that you can trust to guide you accurately and wisely. You will be aided in all your decision-making by both an internal and external validation, two absolutely trustworthy voices in harmony.

Whenever you ask yourself a question, you immediately begin your search for the answer. Trust that your psychic self will respond with the information you need—but remember, it may be given in the language of dreams, images, impressions and symbols and you need to add your own wisdom to interpret those images.

When you trust your intuition, you will feel secure because you will be reconnected with your long-lost skill. It will be like finding an old friend again.

Intuition or psychic sense isn't logical reasoning. It is the opposite. Suddenly, you will find that you just *know*. Immediately, instantly, you will know what is right for you. When that happens you can relax, sure about whatever the judgment is you have made for yourself and your life. Perhaps for the first time you will find that you can put faith in what your own eyes see, what your own ears hear, what your emotions tell you is happening in your own world.

As you have more psychic experiences and begin to accept them as part of your normal life, you will feel better, more energized. You will be in tune with nature, your very being will resonate with the music of the spheres.

Mae often talked of "the pulsing life of the universe, the music of the spheres," and she always made it seem as if she saw and felt it, that it was something very real to her. Real in ways that appeared very different from the abstract way other people talked about their jobs, or science, or technology, or even about their religion. She said, "You will realize that you have rediscovered magic, that intangible something that may have been missing from your life. Something you couldn't name but something you have been searching for."

When you find enjoyment in the reliability of your own psychic power you will have such increased energy, a feeling of happiness, vitality and vibrancy. You will feel optimistic about the future. As your optimism grows, much about your life will improve. Your face will glow, you will find that your immune system is enhanced, and your relationships will expand and deepen. Unexpectedly, new people will come into your life who will help you to find new truths. Once you have a deep conviction that you can rely on your own intuition you will be encouraged to meet life's challenges and you will be able to do so in a more playful, creative and innovative style. *What fun you are going to have!*

Do you remember when you were a child listening to bedtime stories, tales that always happened in enchanted places? You could close your eyes and imagine a castle, a land, a creature, one that could delight and charm you? You would be transported to a world where you could be so jubilant at the pleasure of it. If you have ever dreamed you were flying, only to wake up and find that you were stuck to the bed, you know that every one of us needs to be able to fly.

One of Mae's favorite lines was, When we sleep, (as Thoreau wrote), we could be delivered into a place where "when we dream we also hear and feel the wind among the pines." That joy in your dreams can be brought into the wide-awake world, your everyday world. You will find it will bring with it a sense of completeness and that your reality is now more fulfilling than you ever thought it could be.

The Responsibilities

You must not be seduced by psychic powers. Don't think that now, if you have reconnected with your psychic gift it means that you are unique, or even chosen, because it doesn't. You have to recognize these abilities for what they really are—a part of the world that is available to everyone. With their access comes responsibility, and only when you know that will you be a true psychic, attuned to the gift, comfortable and open to it. The power that comes with paranormal experiences can be very seductive. Treat it with the utmost respect. Don't be lured into experimenting with the lives and fortunes of others.

For 2,000 years physicians entering the practice of medicine have taken the Hippocratic Oath, by which they swear that they will do the patient no harm. A healer should live in a manner that is consistent with one's spiritual and ethical ideals, to live the Golden Rule every moment of life.

Many people are anxious to be psychic but haven't given much thought to what they would do if they were. If you faithfully observe the message in the Hippocratic Oath and the Golden Rule, principles for human behavior which have stood the test of time, then, when you access your psychic powers, you will never do harm by listening to your psychic voice.

For those who are interested in becoming healers it is a tremendous responsibility, one that should not be taken lightly. Psychic healing is another, very separate part of the psychic experience and to become such a healer is not a simple task. You must look into your heart. Examine the parts of your personality that may be power-seeking rather than therapeutic. Interference in another's energy field must be done with integrity and honesty, and should be done only if you have disciplined yourself to have a higher, caring motive.

The Holistic Nurses' Association endorses classes for nurses who wish to add therapeutic touch to their work with patients. All of their literature and their teaching indicates that such work should be an adjunct to other healing modalities, not a *replacement* of them. Be careful. If you feel that you have some need to heal or that you can bring healing energies to others, know that you can only *assist* with the transmission of energy. Perhaps you can increase the individuals' ability to heal themselves, but you should never think that you can *cure* them. Psychic healing is a great gift, one that constantly demands your respect in its use.

The Meaning of the Paranormal

If you now have savored even the tiniest experience of what the expanded world of being psychic is like, what does it mean?

There have been thousands of reports of individuals for whom a psychic experience was life-altering. People from all walks of life (in the diverse worlds of medicine, painting, photography, music, drama, literature, films, architecture, politics, military life, athletics, science and religion) have made significant changes in their lives and in the lives of others when they had an inspirational experience brought to them through their sixth sense. Writers have reported that the whole plot of a best-selling novel was revealed to them in a dream; scientists have suddenly found the answer to a complex problem, one struggled with for years. Musicians have heard the score of a song in their heads as they drove along the highway.

Go ahead, experience synchronicities, dream. It could happen
to you, too.

The Future

Simplistically, we might say that the paranormal is the way of
the future. The gigantic changes occurring in science, the shrinking
of the globe because of telecommunications and ecological concerns, the reawakening of interest in spirituality and advances in
medicine—all appear to be leading us to a new way of viewing the
world in the next millennium.

As we come to realize that the now recognized boundaries of
space and time may be obsolete, the very way we understand how
the world works may have to be revised. Perhaps we can understand
the universal mind as a large information storage hologram and
actual reality as a vast space filled with many different kinds of
oscillating fields, all interacting with each other. In this last one
hundred years we have found that matter and energy were the same
and interchangeable; in the next one hundred years we may find
it also true that our universe is an interlocking web of fields, each
pulsating at its own rate but in harmony with all the others; that
human consciousness can learn to expand and interact with these
many fields of force so that we can tune into the reality of the
world as it actually *is*.

It is known that major corporations are using psychics to aid
in decision-making and management while attorneys have called
upon them for help in negotiations and jury selection. Even financial
planners are consulting psychics in market forecasting. There is
even a psychic market newsletter which many investors rely on.

Psychic healing, traveling to distant planets, operating equipment of all kinds with our minds, communicating over long distances instantly, all those things that have been thought to be no
more than science fiction may soon become commonplace.

It has been reported that Sony Corporation is conducting

research into alternative medicine, X-ray vision, telepathy and other forms of extra-sensory perception. It is rumored that large corporations such as AT&T and Microsoft are exploring commercial applications using employees with psychic skills. Although our government also denies it, there are rumors that they continue research into psychic spying and warfare. As these skills reveal their usefulness, it is no longer farfetched to think that in the next century job descriptions may include the ability to read auras or communicate telepathically.

You may find that increasing your psychic abilities improves your health, decreases stress, aids in your decision-making and gives you more control over your life. You will find that your potential is greater, you may cry and laugh more often, you will become more spontaneous, your creativity will soar as you develop your skills, you will be energized and increasingly positive, your perspective on the world will be balanced and enhanced. You will be able to follow your hunches, make better decisions about how to handle your own finances, know others a little better and understand how to deal with them more positively. You will select a life partner who is right for you, be able to decide what to do with your life, what directions you should take for your future. You will be healthier, stronger and much, much wiser.

Be positive. Use your power well and it can add richness, depth, color, excitement and a great new dimension to your life. When you approach the ability to be psychic in a spirit of love and caring, not as a means of power over others, when you use your talent as a vehicle for correct action and service to others, your intentions are proper.

It is possible to be psychic without any religious or spiritual beliefs, but there should always be an ethical component to your actions. The beauty of accepting the paranormal is that you can view it as a way to see the enlarged world around you, a way to make a spiritual or religious connection to the Universe—or both.

If you find that psychic experiences bring you joy, if you have been yearning for a connectedness with deeper meaning—you will find that increasing your time spent in relaxation, meditation, or focused awareness, and in keeping a dream journal will be transforming. Meditation helps you to stop the constant static of your active mind and increases your ability to connect to the power. Keeping a dream journal makes you more conscious of your dreams, and as a consequence you will dream more vividly and be better able to recall those dreams. Dream recall will soon bring you to that connection with the collective or universal consciousness. These are the things that will open you to the visions, dreams, feelings and emotions of the psychic experiences you seek. You will find that by reading, dreaming and meditating you will suddenly connect with a new experience that will, by its very synchronicity, open up new paths. You will find new people in your life, and new experiences that will increase your intuitive skills. You will suddenly discover that you are hearing or reading about workshops and lectures that make connecting with the psychic realm easier and easier.

Psychologists have said that we only use about 10 percent of our minds and our abilities. Many of those abilities have been stifled since childhood. The remaining 90 percent goes silently along, unused, just waiting to be called into action. Call on that waiting ability and use it.

For thirty days:

1. Relax and meditate—five minutes a day is a good beginning.
2. Visualize—create a safe and beautiful place for yourself and improve on your mental ability to move people and things around in this space. Always include emotion.
3. Focus and observe the world around you, using all your senses.
4. Keep a dream journal—even if you only jot down dream fragments, you are beginning. Look for personal symbolism, use your emotional responses and free association to interpret them.
5. Observe—start with the synchronicities that are sure to

occur. You will soon see your psychic abilities, which were only dormant, blossom and grow.

It seems appropriate here to recall that Einstein, who often said that our understanding of how the universe worked was far from complete, wrote: "The most beautiful and most profound emotion we can experience is the sensation of the mystical. It is the sower of all true science. He to whom this emotion is a stranger, who can no longer wonder and stand rapt in awe, is as good as dead."

So enter into the connection with the vast, ever-unfolding universe that is out there, waiting for you to contact it. Take this journey. Venturing into it can be a joyous experience.

And as my mother Mae would tell you, "You can rediscover your own extraordinary abilities. Enjoy them, let them enrich your life and revel in it! Let your psychic skills expand. Empower yourself and find your psychic self!"

BIBLIOGRAPHY

Achterberg, Jan. *Imagery and Healing: Shamanism & Modern Medicine.* Boston, MA & London, England: New Science Library, 1985.

Al Huang, Chungliang and Lynch, Jerry. *Thinking Body, Dancing Mind. Tao Sports.* New York, NY: Bantam Books, 1992.

Bagnall, O. *The Origins and Properties of the Human Aura.* New York, NY: University Books, Inc., 1970.

Bailey, Alice A. *Esoteric Healing.* Albany, NY: Lucis Trust Publishing Co. 1984.

Barnett, L. *The Universe and Dr. Einstein.* New York, NY: Bantam Books, 1979.

Bentov, Itzhak. *Stalking the Wild Pendulum: On the Mechanics of Consciousness.* Rochester, VT: Destiny Books, 1988.

Brugh, Joy. *Joy's Way.* Los Angeles, CA: Jeremy P. Tarcher, Inc., 1979.

Bohm, David. *Causality & Chance in Modern Physics.* Philadelphia: Univ. of Pennsylvania Press, 1996.

Bohm, David. *Wholeness and the Implicate Order.* New York, NY: Routledge, 1981.

Boss, M. *The Analysis of Dreams.* New York, NY: Philosophical Library, 1958.

Brennan, Barbara. *Hands of Light.* New York, NY: Pleiades Books, 1987.

Burr, H. S. and Northrop, F.S.G. "Evidence for the Existence of an

Electrodynamic Field in the Living Organisms." *Proceedings of the National Academy of Sciences of the United States of America.* Vol. 24 (1939).

Campbell, Joseph. *The Power of Myth* with Bill Moyers. New York, NY: Doubleday, 1988.

Capra, Fritjof. *The Tao of Physics.* Berkeley, CA: Shambhala, 1975.

Carlson, Richard & Shield, Benjamin. *Healers on Healing.* Los Angeles, CA: Jeremy P. Tarcher, Inc. 1989.

Chopra, Deepak. *Ageless Body, Timeless Mind.* New York, NY: Harmony Books, 1993.

———. *Quantum Healing.* New York, NY: Bantam Books, 1989.

Cooper, Paulette and Paul Noble. *The 100 Top Psychics in America.* New York, NY: Simon & Schuster, Inc., 1996.

Crichton, Michael. *Jurassic Park.* New York, NY: Random House, 1990.

Csikszentmihalyi, Mihaly. *Creativity: Flow and the Psychology of Discovery and Invention.* NY: HarperCollins Pub., Inc., 1996.

———. *Flow: The Psychology of Optimal Experience.* New York, NY: Harper & Row Publishers, Inc., 1990.

Cushing, James T. and Ernan Mullin. *Philosophical Consequences of Quantum Theory: Reflections on Bell's Theorem.* South Bend, IN: Univ. of Notre Dame Press, 1989.

De Becker, Gavin. *The Gift of Fear: Survival Signals that Protect Us from Violence.* Boston: Little, Brown and Company, 1997.

Dossey, B., L. Keegan, C. E., Gkluzzeta, L. G. Kolkmeir. *Holistic Nursing: A Handbook for Practice.* Rockville, MD: Aspen Publishers, Inc., 1988.

Day, Laura. *Practical Intuition.* New York, NY: Villard Books, 1996.

Duncan, Lois and William Roll. *Psychic Connections: A Journey into the Mysterious World of Psi.* New York, NY: Delacorte Press, 1995.

Dunne, J. W. *An Experiment with Time.* New York, NY: Humanities Publishing, 1958.

Fulghum, Robert. *All I Really Need to Know I Learned in Kindergarten: Uncommon Thoughts on Common Things.* New York, NY: Villard Books, 1988.

Faraday, Ann. *The Dream Game.* New York, NY: Harper & Row, 1974.

Foundation for Inner Peace. *A Course in Miracles.* Tiburon, CA: Foundation, 1985.

Garfield, Patricia. *Creative Dreaming.* New York, NY: Simon & Schuster, 1995.

Gerber, Richard. *Vibrational Medicine*. Santa Fe, NM: Bear & Co., 1988.

Geller, Uri. *Uri Geller's Mindpower Kit*. New York, NY: Penguin Books, 1996.

Grad, B., R.F. Cadoret, and G.I. Paul. "An Unorthodox Method of Treatment of Wound Healing in Mice," *International Journal of Parapsychology, 3 (2)* 5-19 1961.

Gravelle, Karen, and Robert Rivlin. *Deciphering the Senses*. New York, NY: Simon & Schuster, 1984.

Hastings, Arthur. *With the Tongues of Men and Angels: A Study of Channeling*. Cambridge Univ. Press, 1991.

James, William. *Prgamatism: A New Name for Old Ways of Thinking*. Harvard Univ. Press, 1975.

Jamison, Kay Redfield. *An Unquiet Mind*. New York, NY: Simon & Schuster, 1993.

Jung, Carl G. *Man and His Symbols*. GardenCity, NJ: Doubleday & Company, 1969.

———. *Memories, Dreams, Reflections*. New York, NY: Random House, 1965.

Kovach, Sue. *Hidden Files—Law Enforcement's True Case Stories of the Unexplained and Paranormal*. Chicago: Contemporary Books, 1997.

Krieger, Dolores. *Accepting Your Power to Heal: The Personal Practice of Therapeutic Touch*. Santa Fe, NM: Bear & Company Publishing, 1993.

———. *Living the Therapeutic Touch*. NY: Dodd, Meade & Company, 1987.

———. "The relationship of touch with intent to help or heal subject; in-vivo values: A study of personalized interaction," in *Proceedings of the Ninth American Nurses' Association Nursing Research Conference*. Kansas City, MO: American Nurses' Association 1973.

———. *Therapeutic Touch: How to Use Your Hands to Help or to Heal*. New Jersey: Prentice-Hall, Inc., 1979.

Kunz, Dora and S. Karagulla. *Chakras and the Human Energy Field*. Wheaton, IL: Theosophical Society in America, 1989.

Le Shan, L. *The Medium, the Mystic, and the Physicist*. New York, NY: Ballantine Books, 1966.

Lyons, Arthur. *The Blue Sense: Psychic Detectives and Crime*. New York, NY: Mysterious Press, 1991.

MacLaine, Shirley. *Out on a Limb*. New York, NY: Bantam Books, 1984.

Mann, W. E. *Orgone, Reich and Eros.* New York, NY: Simon & Schuster, 1973.

McGee, Charles T., and Effie Poy Yew Chow. *Oigong: Miracle Healing from China.* Coeur d'Alene, ID: Medipress, 1996.

McBride, Joseph. *Steven Spielberg: A Biography.* New York, NY, Simon & Schuster, 1997.

Mercado, Walter. *Beyond the Horizon: Visions of the New Millinnium.* New York, NY: Warner Books, 1997.

Monroe, Robert A. *Journeys Out of the Body.* New York, NY: Doubleday, 1977.

Morehouse, David. *Psychic Warrior: Inside the CIA's Stargate Program.* New York, NY: St. Martin's Press, 1996.

Myer-Czetli, Nancy. *Silent Witness: The Story of a Psychic Detective.* New York, NY: Coral Publishing Group, 1993.

Myss, Caroline, PhD. *Anatomy of the Spirit: The Seven Stages of Power and Healing.* New York, NY: Harmony Books, 1996.

Nhat Hanh, Thich. *The Blooming of a Lotus: Guided Meditation Exercises for Healing and Transformation.* MA: Beacon Press, 1993.

Ostrander, Sheila and Lynn Schroeder. *Psychic Discoveries Behind the Iron Curtain.* Englewood Cliffs, NJ: Prentice-Hall, 1970.

Radin, Dean. *The Conscious Universe: The Scientific Truth of Psychic Phenomena.* New York, NY: HarperCollins Publishers, Inc., 1997.

Randi, James. *Flim-Flam!: Psychics, ESP, Unicorns and Other Delusions.* Buffalo, NY: Prometheus Books, 1982.

Rhine, L. *Hidden Channels of the Mind.* New York, NY: William Sloan, 1961.

Sagan, Carl. *The Demon-Haunted World: Science as a Candle in the Dark.* New York, NY: Ballantine Books, 1996.

Sark. *A Creative Companion: How to Free Your Creative Spirit.* Berkeley, CA: Celestial Arts, 1991.

Sharamon, Shalila & Baginski, Bodo J. *The Chakra-Handbook* Wilmot: WI: 1991.

Siegel, Bernie. *Love, Medicine and Miracles.* New York, NY: Harper & Row, 1986.

Sinclair, Upton. *Mental Radio.* New York, NY: TimeLife, 1991.

Sparks, Laurance. *Self-hypnosis: A Conditioned Response Technique.* New York, NY: Grune & Stratton, Inc., 1962.

Stekel, W. *The Interpretation of Dreams.* New York, NY: Grosset and Dunlap, 1962.

Storr, Anthony. *Music and the Mind.* New York, NY: Ballantine Books, 1992.

Sugrue, Thomas. *There is a River: The Story of Edgar Cayce.* New York, NY: Dell Publishing Co., Inc., 1945.

Swann, Ingo. *To Kiss Earth Goodbye.* New York, NY: Dell, 1975.

Targ, Russell, and Keith Harary. *The Mind Race: Understanding and Using Psychic Abilities.* New York, NY: Ballantine Books, 1984.

Tart, Charles T. *Open Mind, Discriminating Mind.* Chicago, IL: Univ. of Chicago Press, 1976.

Van de Castle, Robert, PhD. *Our Dreaming Mind.* New York, NY: Random House, 1994.

White, John and S. Krippner. *Future Science: Life Energies and the Physics of Paranormal Phenomena.* New York, NY: Doubleday, 1977.

Wise, Anna. *The High-Performance Mind: Mastering Brainwaves for Insight, Healing and Creativity.* New York, NY: Tarcher/Putnam Books, 1995.

Zdenek, Marilee. *The Right-Brain Experience: An Intimate Program to Free the Powers of Your Imagination.* New York, NY: McGraw-Hill Book Co., 1983.